The Road from Serfdom

ROBERT SKIDELSKY

The Road from Serfdom

The Economic and Political Consequences of the End of Communism

ALLEN LANE
THE PENGUIN PRESS

To David Calleo

from whom I have learnt, and with whom I have argued,
over many years of friendship

ALLEN LANE THE PENGUIN PRESS
Published by the Penguin Group
Penguin Books USA Inc., 375 Hudson Street,
New York, New York 10014, U.S.A.
Penguin Books Ltd, 27 Wrights Lane,
London W8 5TZ, England
Penguin Books Australia Ltd, Ringwood,
Victoria, Australia
Penguin Books Canada Ltd, 10 Alcorn Avenue,
Toronto, Ontario, Canada M4V 3B2
Penguin Books (N.Z.) Ltd, 182–190 Wairau Road,
Auckland 10, New Zealand

Penguin Books Ltd, Registered Offices:
Harmondsworth, Middlesex, England

First American edition
Published in 1996 by Viking Penguin,
a division of Penguin Books USA Inc.

10 9 8 7 6 5 4 3 2 1

Copyright © Robert Skidelsky, 1995
All rights reserved

Originally published in Great Britain under the title *The World After Communism.*

LIBRARY OF CONGRESS CATALOGING IN PUBLICATION DATA
Skidelsky, Robert Jacob Alexander.
   The Road from serfdom / Robert Skidelsky.
      p.   cm.
   Previously published: The world after Communism. New York: Macmillan.
   Includes bibliographical references and index.
   ISBN 0-7139-9122-4
   1. Post-communism. 2. Collectivism—History—20th century.
I. Title.
HX44.5.S55   1996
338.9—dc20   95-38459

This book is printed on acid-free paper.
∞

Printed in the United States of America
Set in Janson Text

CONTENTS

ACKNOWLEDGEMENTS

I am deeply grateful to my research assistant, Julian Kenny. He has helped shape the structure and argument of this book over many months and conversations. I would also like to thank Liam Halligan. For over three years now – ever since he took my 'Age of Keynes' course at Warwick University – we have been talking about economics, political economy and the role of economists, and much of what appears here reflects the impact of those discussions, as well as his probing criticisms of earlier drafts of the text. Others who had read and pronounced on draft chapters are Barry Buzan, David Carlton, Danny Finkelstein, Jean Floud, Charles Jones and Larry Siedentop. Celestine Bohlen, Christopher Granville, Vladimir Mau and Andrea Richter were all extraordinarily helpful to me in Moscow. I would like to thank them all.

I am deeply indebted to the Wolfson Foundation for giving me a grant to write this book, to Warwick University for giving me time off to do it, and to the Social Market Foundation for providing me with facilities and such a congenial intellectual atmosphere. I would also like to thank the staff of the House of Lords Library for their unfailing helpfulness to Julian Kenny and myself.

Finally, my thanks go to my family – my wife, Augusta, and our three children, Edward, William and Juliet – who have had to put up with considerable grumpiness, as well as some obsessional conversation, as I struggled to finish the book over the summer. Both Edward and William have helped me with ideas, and William also with research on Russia.

The faults are all mine. For the American edition, I have taken the opportunity to correct slips, strengthen the argument in one or two places and update events since the fall of Communism. The future is open-ended. The only thing we can certainly expect is the unexpected. Our own attitude of mind, optimistic or pessimistic, and the acts which flow from it, will affect what happens. This essay is a modest contribution to an optimistic outlook.

—ROBERT SKIDELSKY, *14 July 1995*

INTRODUCTION

The collapse of Communism was greeted with a triumphalism appropriate to a crushing military victory. The failure of Communism and all other forms of collectivism seemed to vindicate capitalism and political democracy, and to remove any systematic obstacles to their universal adoption. The optimists looked forward to the reconstruction of post-Communist societies on Western lines and their incorporation into a Western-led international order. A world integrated by trade and democracy would not only soar to unimagined heights of prosperity but would also realize the nineteenth-century liberal dream of universal peace.

This euphoric moment soon succumbed to the realities of the 'transition'. The optimists were succeeded by the pessimists, who came from all political camps and none. Socialists, defeated in the West, attacked the lunacy of imposing 'free-market economics' on the East. Cold War warriors, deprived of their old constituency, warned of new threats to world peace. The collapse of the over-arching imperial structures of the Cold War would release not the cosmopolitan Utopia but the historical passions and enmities which the bipolar hegemony had kept under control. The future was written in the bloody disintegration of Yugoslavia. Pessimists of the world united in their belief that the new situation was, if anything, worse than the old.

The pessimists had some good points. The dislocations involved in the collapse of Communism were far more horrendous than those which had accompanied earlier liberalizing moves in the 'First' and 'Third' Worlds. The transition to post-Communism had to be attempted in societies whose economies, legal systems and political and social life had been damaged and deformed by decades of oppression and mismanagement. Moreover, there was no ready-made world order into which the post-Communist societies could slot, but a set of transnational Western institutions bound to unravel with the end of the Cold War which had created them. Nor was there a single Western model of economic success, merely a collection of capitalist economies, themselves undergoing the strains of structural transformation, and burdened with high unemployment. The pessimists also made the more fundamental, and familiar, point that the liberal Utopia could not be realized, because it was a-historical. It ignored not just the problems of the transition but also the permanent realities of social and international conflict.

In part, these violently opposed assessments of the future rest on the weight given to short-run and long-run factors. The short run is always a sea of troubles, in which optimism is liable to drown. We should look to the permanent, not temporary, effects of the collapse of Communism. The trouble is that the long run is a succession of short runs. Everything which happens in one period forms the historical material of the next. What happens now is not a rite of passage, but will affect the direction of the passage.

The deeper question is whether societies can transcend their history. Are we bound to collapse back into collectivism and corporatism, or can we go beyond these stale doctrines? Is the European Union destined to disintegrate with the end of the Cold War, or is it a new form of political life which has successfully domesticated age-old national hatreds? Such questions cannot be answered in the abstract. The answers depend on our own state of mind. The underlying mind-set of the pessimists is one of *regret*. Many, perhaps most, on the Left regret the defeat of Communism, however disfigured it was in practice, because it marks the defeat of the socialist project. It is not a socialism purged of its imperfections which is arising from the ashes of Communism, but a capitalism reborn; and the Left do not wish it well. Many conservatives regret the passing of the Cold War, because they fear that without the discipline it imposed their societies will fall to pieces, old demons will be let loose, and the world will revert to anarchy.

The pessimists are a wearying lot. They tend to say in advance that nothing new will work. When nevertheless it does work somewhere, they produce subtle arguments to prove it will not work anywhere else. I am an optimist. I regard the end of Communism, the rolling back of the frontiers of the state, the globalization of economic intercourse, as the most hopeful turn of the historical screw which has happened since 1914. I do not believe that societies are destined to repeat their histories. But neither are they likely to jump into a world of non-history. This leaves liberal statesmanship a more substantial task than many optimists suppose. It is not just to dismantle dysfunctional systems, releasing new energies, but so to manage the transition that the job can be completed. Optimists must not give up their ideals, but must navigate well in the storm.

What follows is an essay in political economy, not international relations. This is not to say that the international relations of the post-Communist world will not be full of problems, but the problems will be negotiable as long as we get the politics and economics right. I try to explain how we have reached post-Communism, not by means of historical narrative, but in terms of a single organizing idea which I call the rise and fall of collectivism. Collectivism – the belief that the state knows better than the market, and can improve on the spontaneous tendencies of civil society, if necessary by suppressing them – has been the most egregious error of the twentieth century. Its extreme manifestations were in Communism and Fascism, but it was also seen in the authoritarian state-led industrialization policies of many developing countries, and large traces have been evident in the industrial and social policies of most developed economies. My contention is that this belief in the superior wisdom of the state breeds pathologies which deform, and at the limit destroy, the political economies based on it.

This explanatory scheme makes a pattern of twentieth-century history. It is not the only possible pattern, but it is the only one which can account for the *worldwide* character of the shift in political economy which took place in the 1980s, which otherwise is left as a series of disconnected events, fortuitously linked in time. We need, I think, to try to understand why it was that practically all governments, the world over, started to dismantle their collectivist economies, or the collectivized parts of their economies, at roughly the same time, and under the same general inspiration.

The history of the rise and fall of collectivism shows that people want security as well as freedom, and that it is all too easy for idealists, intellectuals and adventurers to force populations into an iron cage of bondage in the name of providing security against real or imagined ills. So any durable 'constitution of liberty' has to satisfy both the desire for liberty and the need for security. The nearest we have come to satisfying both desires this century was during the so-called 'golden age' of the 1950s and 1960s – the twentieth-century equivalent of the nineteenth century's 'age of equipoise'. It seemed, briefly, that the Soviet Union under Khrushchev might be capable of establishing its own 'constitution of liberty'; but its Marxist-Leninist ideology made the Soviet system unreformable. Also, the Western political economy congealed in the 1970s into a collectivist mould, against which the 1980s saw a sharp reaction back to economic liberalism. This was shared by those developing countries which abandoned their state-led industrialization policies for integration into the world market.

We are thus living through a period of transition. In addition to the expert navigation which will surely be needed to steer us through this passage without too much damage to our hopes, we will need to give urgent attention to the concept and content of a 'rule of law' for governments which will prevent a backsliding into the collectivist morass from which we are now extricating ourselves. With the collapse of Communism we return to what the Czech prime minister Václav Klaus calls the 'enduring question of how far the state should regulate the lives of free and responsible individuals'.

CHAPTER ONE

'WE WILL BURY YOU'

In 1961 the first secretary of the Communist Party of the Soviet Union, Nikita Khrushchev, made an extraordinary speech. He predicted that within ten years the Soviet Union would overtake America in total industrial production, and within twenty-five years would outstrip its rival in wealth per head of population. 'We will bury you,' Khrushchev told the West. Nearly half a century after the Bolshevik seizure of power in October 1917, Khrushchev was speaking for a revolutionary state apparently confident of its own future and of its dominant position in the future of the world. How far Khrushchev believed what he said is open to doubt. But his truculent rhetoric was taken at face value in the West. When President Kennedy came to London in June 1961, fresh from confronting Khrushchev in Vienna, he told Britain's Conservative prime minister, Harold Macmillan, 'they are no longer frightened of aggression. They have at least as powerful nuclear forces as the West. They have interior lines. *They have a buoyant economy and will soon outmatch Capitalist society in the race for materialist wealth.*' Macmillan agreed.[1]

Khrushchev was also speaking for a state which seemed to have shed the worst features of its Stalinist past. In his speech to the Twentieth Congress of the Communist Party on 20 February 1956, Khrushchev had not only denounced the crimes of Stalin but had also acknowledged the possibility of a parliamentary route to socialism. This speech, whose effect was only partly undone by the brutal Soviet suppression of the Hungarian uprising later that year, was greeted with tremendous excitement by Western socialist intellectuals. The Soviet Union and its 'model' were becoming respectable again.

Khrushchev's threat did not *seem* like an idle boast. The Soviet Union claimed an annual growth rate of 10 per cent between 1950 and 1960. America's Central Intelligence Agency halved this. The real figure was about 7 per cent – still well over double the United States', and faster than that of any European country. This was Communism's peak decade. No one could know that from 1960 Soviet growth would slow down, and a decade and a half after that go into reverse. Nor could they know that China's 'Great Leap Forward', started by Mao Tse-tung in 1959, would turn out to be a disastrous and murderous fiasco.

Khrushchev's *economic* boasting hit the West at its most vulnerable point. The West's core value – what in fact defined 'the West' – was belief in political and religious freedom. It was the suppression of these freedoms in Eastern Europe which had started the Cold War. But the West was much less sure about economic freedom. Well into the 1970s there was a fear, which for some was a hope, that Communism might ultimately be shown to work better than capitalism, on the double test of economic growth and equality. Many in the West wanted to believe Khrushchev, for, if what he said was true, the case for a non-coercive form of socialism was securely established. And anti-Communists were aware of the force of the Communist example on the developing countries of Latin America, Asia and Africa. The de-Stalinized Soviet Russia of Nikita Khrushchev posed, for the first time since the 1930s, an ideological as well as a military challenge. If capitalism on its own could not outgrow and outlast Communism, it had to be geared up to do so by state intervention.

It was Russia's military challenge which set alarm bells ringing in the Pentagon. On 4 October 1957 the Russians launched *Sputnik*, the first satellite, into space; on 12 April 1961 Yuri Gagarin became the first man (Soviet man!) to orbit the earth. 'America has lost a battle more important and greater than Pearl Harbor,' Dr Edward Teller, inventor of the H-bomb, told a nationwide TV audience. Senator Lyndon Johnson's adviser, George Reedy, thought that 'the race for control of the universe has started'.[2] In 1957 Governor Orval Faubus of Arkansas sent in his National Guard to stop the racial desegregation of schools; President Dwight D. Eisenhower eventually sent in US paratroopers to enforce desegregation. 'The tale carried faster than drum signals across black Africa,' noted Eisenhower's speech-writer.[3] The Soviet Union had scored a major propaganda victory: however many millions of its own people it had murdered, it was not racialist or colonialist. Early in 1959 Castro's Communists seized power in Cuba, less than a hundred miles from the coast of Florida. In September 1962 reconnaissance flights showed that Soviet missiles were being installed on Cuba. A nuclear as well as a revolutionary dagger was pointed at the Americas.

The secret Gaither Report, presented to Eisenhower by his strategic experts on 7 November 1957, painted a gloomy picture of a nation losing ground militarily, technologically and ideologically to a worldwide Communist offensive, backed by 'rocketing Soviet military might and . . . a powerful, growing Soviet economy and technology'.[4] In his 1959 best-seller *The Uncertain Trumpet*, General Maxwell Taylor, former US Army chief of staff, warned that from 1961 the military balance would shift decisively against the United States unless 'we take drastic action now'. This became one of the texts of the 1960 presidential election campaign. John F. Kennedy, the successful candidate, fought his campaign on rearmament: 'We will mould our strength and become first again . . . I want the world to wonder not what Mr Khrushchev is doing. I want them to wonder what the United States is doing.'[5] The subsequent revelation that the missile gap favoured Washington, not Moscow, did little to lessen the sense of a nation and system under threat.

The origins of what Kennedy called the 'struggle for supremacy between two conflicting ideologies: freedom under God versus ruthless, godless tyranny' go back, of course, all the way to the Bolshevik Revolution of 1917, which provoked America's first response in Woodrow Wilson's championship of national self-determination. However, with the United States and the Soviet Union both in isolation in the 1930s, centre stage was occupied by Europe's 'civil war', which pitted the Fascist powers, Germany and Italy (distantly allied to Japan), against the Western imperial democracies, Britain and France. Ironically what this struggle was partly about was how best to organize Europe's defence against Communism. What it showed was that Fascism could not be the ideological standard-bearer of anti-Communism. It was the actions of Germany and Japan, in 1941, in globalizing the European war, which eliminated the democratic versus Fascist sub-plot – and indeed Europe's by now diseased hegemony – and brought American capitalism and Russian Communism face to face across the stricken body of Germany in 1945.

In its institutionalized form the Cold War started with a series of rapidly escalating moves and countermoves by the USA and the Soviet Union from 1946 onwards which, by 1949, had cemented the division of Europe into two political and military systems between which there was, as Churchill said, an 'iron curtain'. In 1949 the Soviet Union tested its first atom bomb, and the iron curtain was reinforced by the 'nuclear stalemate'. In the same year the Communists won the civil war in China, in 1950 North Korea invaded South Korea, and the struggle between 'freedom' and 'Communism' became worldwide, with Asia, later Latin America and Africa, forming the fluid frontiers. The United States began rearmament in 1947 when President Truman announced a build-up in the defence budget from $13.5 billion a year to $50 billion over a five-year period. 'American diplomacy, defence budgets and military reach exploded across the globe in the aftermath of the invasion [of South Korea], as US taxpayers and Congress alike gave the unstinted political support the strategic planners had hitherto sought with only limited success.'6

In understanding the Cold War, we need to be constantly aware of what each side believed it was protecting from what. Its origins are often blamed on misperception: the United States allegedly misinterpreted Stalin's defensive thrusts in Eastern Europe between 1946 and 1948 as the spearhead of a world Communist offensive; Stalin mistakenly believed US capitalism was bent on world domination. It is not clear where the misconception lies. The US did want a capitalist world, the USSR a Communist one. They both conducted their foreign policy to secure what the Soviets called a 'favourable correlation of forces'. Both sides may have been wrong about the willingness of the other to pursue its aims by reckless use of force. For Stalin, occupation of Eastern Europe was insurance against a rearmed Germany. But it has to be remembered that, when the Cold War started, Germany was defenceless and the whole of Western Europe was virtually disarmed. Far more realistically menacing to Western democrats was a victorious Soviet army of 3 million men, with huge Communist parties in France and Italy which took their orders from Moscow. The inexcusable error of some Western historians and analysts had been to treat the values and logics of the two sides as symmetrical.[7] This has the effect of giving Stalin a 'cause' which may claim respect, if not allegiance. The essential point is that the Soviets were quite wrong to believe that capitalism meant enslavement, whereas the Americans were quite right to believe that Stalinist Communism did. The ideologies of the two sides, that is, were not of equal value. The Communist rulers were defending not Russia nor even socialism, but their own absolute power. Had Stalin been prepared to dilute Communism with political freedom, he would have had a cause, and the history of the world might have been very different.

At the height of the Cold War the talk was of the free world versus Communism. But the Communist world, sometimes known as the 'Second World', was much more compact than the 'free world'. Geographically it dominated the Eurasian heartland. Its political economy was also clear-cut, being based on public ownership, central planning and party-state dictatorship. This created an image of concentrated strength, which in fact it lacked. Its coordinating institutions, the Warsaw Pact and COMECON, did not, however, include China.

The 'free world' was much more heterogeneous geographically, politically and economically. The only common feature of non-Communist countries was that their economic systems were based on private ownership. But this meant less than it seemed, because most of the world's poor (the vast majority of its population) lived in 'pre-capitalist' peasant economies, and most non-Communist states had large publicly owned sectors. Within the rhetorical 'free world' there was a capitalist core (sometimes known as the 'First World') which linked the United States to Western Europe across the Atlantic and to Japan across the Pacific. These links were outgrowths of the two wars the United States won between 1941 and 1945, against Germany in Western Europe and against Japan in East Asia. The United States provided its allies with the public goods of security, financial assistance and (more grudgingly) market access needed to rebuild the traditional liberal capitalism which had shrivelled up in the Great Depression of the 1930s. West Germany and Japan were satellites of the United States, which largely reshaped their political and economic institutions, to the great material benefit of their populations. Many who ponder the 'secret' of Japan's economic postwar success may reflect that it started with US spending during the Korean War of 1950–3, was reinforced by the privileged Japanese access to the American market from 1956 onwards, and was given a further boost by the Vietnam War in the mid-1960s. Having grown up in the shadow of the United States, capitalist East Asia by the 1980s included South Korea, Taiwan, Hong Kong, Singapore, Malaysia, Indonesia and the coastal provinces of 'Communist' China. It had become a dynamic economic area in its own right, a source of inspiration but also fear to the stagnating West.

Of the main Western European countries, only Britain, immediately after the war, claimed to be a great power, by virtue of its imperial security and trading links, though these were increasingly marginal to both its security and its prosperity. Until the end of the 1960s, when its resources ran out, Britain played a more than symbolic role in 'containing' Communism in Malaysia, the Middle East and Africa, as junior partner to the United States, possibly at the expense of its own economic performance. Ironically, America's junior partner started off the Cold War period as the most socialist of the capitalist core, the only major Western European country in which a socialist party held power on its own after the war: in France, Italy and Germany the moderate Catholic parties came to dominate politics, sometimes in coalition with socialists. The non-socialist evolution of Western Europe after the war was the combined work of its electorates, the perceived Soviet threat to freedom, and the active involvement of the United States in its reconstruction through Marshall Aid. Marshall Aid was important because the money disbursed was linked to terms and institutions which promoted the 'common marketization' of Western Europe.

But Western Europe was never a mirror image of American capitalism. In the United States socialism was insignificant; this was never true of Western Europe, its birthplace. The socialists and Communists had led the resistance to Fascism in the war. After the war, the socialists played a key role in keeping Western Europe non-Communist. It had by no means been clear that this would be so. In economic and social policy the socialists and Communists were allies. They wanted to end capitalism. They both saw the future in terms of nationalization and national planning. But they split on political method and foreign policy, and this split created the division of Europe. The socialists were democrats. They wanted to introduce socialism incrementally, by parliamentary methods. Had Western European electorates supported them, it is impossible to tell how far socialism in Western Europe would have gone, or what form it would have taken. Because of their commitment to democracy, however, socialists refused to kowtow to Moscow. Stalin's plan was for the socialists and Communists to fuse, leading to 'united-front' governments – especially in France and Italy – which would be subservient to his wishes. The socialists refused the bait and accepted American protection in preference to Soviet dictatorship. This further limited the possibility of socialist construction. The most notable service which Stalinism rendered freedom was to keep Western Europe non-socialist and socialist parties non-Communist. Nevertheless, nationalization of basic industries, economic planning and a welfare state were common features of Western Europe's 'mixed economy'. Many on Left and Right saw it as a European 'third way' between American capitalism and Russian Communism. For the Right had collectivist traditions of its own. France's postwar planning system reflected a return to the *dirigisme* of Louis XIV's chief minister Jean-Baptiste Colbert reinforced by the socialism of Jean Monnet. Germany's social market economy was influenced by home-grown neo-liberalism, political federalism and Catholic corporatism. (Britain helped Germany rebuild a strong trade-union movement.) Italy retained the basic institutions for state intervention established by Fascism. All these elements went into the European Economic Community started in 1958. For many years after the war, Britain's Labour Party was, in theory, the most powerful socialist party of the most powerful state in Western Europe. But its convictions were so diluted by British common-sense, insularity and muddle that it was the despair of its intellectuals, and of all those who hoped for a democratic socialist Europe. By the early 1950s socialism had passed its peak in Western Europe as state-led reconstruction was completed, trade and payments were liberalized, and the capitalist part of the world started to boom under the aegis of the Pax Americana. The same was not true of the poor countries.

The notion of the 'free world' was at its most paradoxical when applied to the so-called 'Third World', as the poor or 'underdeveloped' countries came to be known – Latin America and the collection of non-European states emerging from European colonialism in the 1950s and 1960s. Most of it was ruled by dictators. The Third World first defined itself as such at the Bandung Conference in Indonesia in 1955. What united it was an acute sense of victimhood – a useful rhetorical device for excusing failure and extracting resources from the rich countries. Its ideological core was the notion of state-led industrialization. This drew its inspiration from nineteenth-century economic nationalism, first elaborated in opposition to Britain's 'free-trade imperialism', to which was added a belief in Soviet-style planning. This strategy would enable poor countries to escape from neocolonial domination. The appeal of the Soviet system to poor countries which felt themselves to be victims of imperialism is easy to understand. Under a succession of five-year plans starting in 1929, the Soviet Union had rapidly and massively developed its heavy industrial sector, its mining, its chemical industry, its railways and its network of electrical supply. National mobilization had concentrated the efforts of a primitive and capital-starved economy on the construction of industrial capacity. The costs, it is well known, were very high, amounting to millions of lives. Yet, at the same time, there was undoubtedly rapid economic growth, and in particular an extraordinary amassing of coal- and steel-based industrial might which had enabled the Soviet Union to fling back Hitler's armies. It was an alluring prospect. China in 1949 started on the same route. Independent India's first prime minister, Jawaharlal Nehru, was a devotee of Soviet planning, the principles of which he picked up in England in the 1920s.

The Third World liked to think of itself as 'non-aligned' in the Cold War. This 'neutrality' gave it a limited freedom to play off the two superpowers for aid. When Egypt, in 1956, refused America's terms for building the Aswan Dam, it got the funds from the Soviet Union. This 'non-alignment' was a bit of a myth. The Monroe Doctrine, first enunciated by the United States in 1823 to keep the European powers from meddling in American affairs, was still implicitly enforced to keep Latin America in the Western camp, not mainly by troops, but by money and covert operations. In the struggle for ideological supremacy, the United States had on its side money and technology; the Soviet Union anti-colonialism and poverty. The United States forced the European colonial powers out of the business of policing 'freedom', for which a colonial ideology was plainly unsuited, only to find itself committed to the global support of corrupt and oppressive nationalistic dictatorships. In 1960 Khrushchev, true to Leninist doctrine, proclaimed that capitalist imperialism would be destroyed from the rear by the 'sacred struggle of national liberation'. Kennedy riposted in 1961, 'The great battleground for the defence and expansion of freedom today is Asia, Africa and the Middle East.'[8] As it

entered the 1960s the United States' leadership saw itself faced
with the problem of containing a third wave of Marxist expan-
sionism – after those which followed the First and Second
World Wars – which extended to its own urban ghettoes, at
the precise moment when spectacular Soviet technological
achievements were threatening to defeat it in the arms race.

The way it responded to this perceived threat is the key to
everything which happened subsequently. Anticipating Ronald
Reagan by twenty years, Kennedy put the Soviet Union under
pressure by escalating the arms race. He increased the defence
budget by $3 billion in 1961 and by a further $3 billion in 1962.
Khrushchev responded with a 30 per cent increase in Soviet
military spending. The Kennedy Round of the GATT, started
in 1963, was designed to strengthen the capitalist core by securing multilateral agreement on tariff reductions. Kennedy
also raised the stakes in the Third World by announcing a large
military and civilian aid programme for developing countries.
By forcing the Soviets to compete in arms on the basis of a
much lower national income, Kennedy destroyed Communism's promise to its own people, helped bring about the
downfall of Khrushchev in 1964, and planted the seeds of Communism's own downfall. Of course, he did not achieve these
results unaided. Trapped by their ideology into believing that
Communism was the wave of the future, the Soviets had to keep
up in the arms race, whatever the cost, until the promised revolt
of the Third World would take monopoly capitalism 'from the
rear'. This was the Soviet vision of how the Cold War would
end. Bureaucratic inertia compounded ideological rigidity. As
one US official said, 'When we spend, they spend. When we
slow down, they don't.'

However, the United States, too, paid, and inflicted, a high
price for its simplicities. Even Eisenhower was led to warn in
1960 against the dominance of the 'military-industrial complex'
in the US economy. In 1965, after a brief *détente* which followed
the Cuban missile crisis, the Cold War hotted up in Vietnam,
and President Johnson increased defence spending again, this
time by $13 billion. This came on top of large increases in

federal spending and transfer payments to the states for his 'Great Society' and 'War on Poverty' programmes, which aimed to make the American dream a reality to its urban poor, chiefly blacks. The essential point, though, is that these large expenditure increases were paid for by *cutting* taxes by 10 per cent. Kennedy and Johnson knew that Congress would not agree to raise taxes to pay for increased military and social spending; a tax increase also ran up against their own objection to anything which smacked of socialism – high taxes and socialism being synonyms in the American ideology. Capitalism was to be militarized, but not socialized. Pentagon capitalism would be financed by budget deficits. There was a contradiction at the heart of the American political economy between its Cold War ambitions and a fiscal system based on low taxes – legacies of isolation and the Wild West environment in which American capitalism sprouted.

The circle was squared by the economists who told Kennedy and Johnson that an expansion of aggregate demand by means of budget deficits would raise the growth rate of the US economy sufficiently to pay for both guns and butter. The message was taken up in Britain and on the Continent of Europe. In the 1960s 'growthmanship' became the new economic gospel of the West. In espousing growth, European social democrats found a way of reconciling social demands with the restraints on egalitarianism created by the needs of a capitalist economy. The private sector would be geared up by increased public investment in hospitals, schools, housing, transport systems. The faster growth of the economy would produce additional revenues at unchanged tax rates to pay for more social services – pensions, health care, education, etc. This was Harold Wilson's recipe for faster British growth when he became Labour prime minister in 1964. The Right espoused faster growth through tax cuts as an antidote to socialism; the Left, faster growth through increased public spending as a surrogate for socialism. The Kennedy–Johnson programmes in the United States combined elements of both.

What the vogue for growthmanship indicated was the extraordinary ideological insecurity of capitalism's leaders, in the midst of what was in reality a 'golden age'. Capitalist growth had to be stimulated and planned. This set the mood for state hyperactivism in the 1960s. The political élites of capitalism in the 1960s were convinced that a system of unplanned, unguided economic activity could not meet the moral and economic challenge of the planned systems. The same spirit infected the developing countries, where state spending replaced import controls as the main engine of state-led industrialization.

The costs of competitive overstrain fell on the two blocs in different ways. In the centrally planned economies, which had no private sector, private consumption was rigidly held down to make room for military spending. In the West, the competition between the private and public sectors for resources, as well as between employers and trade unions for shares in the national income, produced inflation.

Under the system of stable, but adjustable, exchange rates set up at Bretton Woods, New Hampshire, in 1944, monetary conditions for all free-world countries were set by the monetary policy of the United States. It was the monetary financing of the US budget deficits in the 1960s which ignited world inflation. The US inflation rate rose from 1 per cent in 1960 to 6 per cent in 1970. But part of the increased money creation in America was 'exported' through the US balance-of-payments deficit, as dollars paid out for imports unrequited by exports found their way into the central banks of other countries and leaked out into the Eurodollar market. The dollar became progressively overvalued against other currencies, particularly the Deutschmark. In 1971 President Nixon sacrificed the fixed-exchange-rate system to American 'growth'. All the major currencies were floating against each other by 1973.

The Hungarian economist János Kornai has distinguished between the 'supply-constrained' economies of Communism and the 'demand-constrained' economies of capitalism. But in practice by the early 1970s both sets of economies were supply-constrained – they were hitting their institutionally determined

production frontiers. Inflationary macroeconomic policy in the
United States produced a world cost explosion – rising domestic wages, rising commodity prices, capped by the fourfold increase in the price of crude oil in 1973–4. Paradoxically,
growthmanship seemed to slow down the real rate of growth.
From the late 1960s the so-called 'misery index' (inflation plus
unemployment) started rising with each business cycle. To try
to stop the relentless rise in costs produced by their own macroeconomic policies, governments imposed wage and price controls. Of course, rigid control of the wages fund had long been
the hallmark of the high-pressure command economies. By the
1970s the quest for growth through budget deficits, started to
'contain Communism', had led capitalist economies to adopt
this central control feature of the collectivist policy.

It was the realization that a fundamental dividing line between free and collectivist economies was being breached – as
well as the breakdown of wage and price controls in practice –
that led to the emergence of the new political economy in the
1980s. Very simply, after 1979 all the main capitalist countries
committed themselves to squeezing inflation out of their systems by tight money policy. The growth of output, wanted and
unwanted, which in the 1970s had been financed by budget
deficits and cheap money, came to a stop, and indeed went into
reverse. Developing countries which had borrowed petrodollars
to finance their growth (mostly at negative real interest rates)
were suddenly faced with crippling debt crises. The 'fiscal crisis'
of the state automatically called into question the long-term
role of the state in the economy. What was, from one point of
view, simply a technical exercise in 'monetarism' was, at a
deeper level, a rediscovery of the values of economic freedom.
The global ideological balance was tilted further in favour of
economic freedom by the emergence of a new region of export-
led capitalist dynamism in East Asia. In retrospect, one can see
that the demonstration effect of East Asia's 'economic miracle'
completely reversed the effect of America's defeat in Vietnam.
It killed stone dead any lingering appeal to the Third World

of the socialist road to development. It marked a stunning defeat for the Communist hope of taking capitalism 'from the rear'.

At the end of the 1970s Western leaders had no means of knowing that collectivism was about to break down in the Communist world. To be sure, there were tell-tale signs of stagnation. But these were masked by the enormous rise in energy prices which benefited the Soviet Union and its allies, because the USSR was a large exporter of energy. The very difficulties which forced the West into painful restructuring enabled the planning system to postpone its day of reckoning. And underneath an increasingly creaking planning façade the expansion of Soviet military budgets and global activity continued unabated. In the late 1970s the Soviets or their surrogates established footholds in Africa, Central America, Laos. The Soviets themselves invaded Afghanistan in 1979. There were new signs of a 'missile gap', both long-range and intermediate: in 1977 the Soviets started installing SS-20 intermediate range missiles in Europe. In a United States traumatized by the Vietnam War, every 'defeat' for US policy – such as the overthrow of the shah in Iran in 1979 by anti-American Islamic fundamentalists – could be seen as a 'gain' for world Communism.

When Ronald Reagan arrived at the White House in 1981 he found 'the fibre of American military muscle was so atrophied that our ability to respond effectively to Soviet military attack was very much in doubt'.[9] It was in this mood that he started the third and last great arms build-up of the Cold War in 1981. Technically, his measures looked like Kennedy's: tax cuts to get the American economy 'moving'; increases in military spending. But the ideological climate was very different from what it had been in Kennedy's day. The Soviet Union was regarded as a serious military threat, but no longer as a serious ideological competitor. Unlike Kennedy and Harold Wilson, Reagan and Margaret Thatcher, the new British prime minister, were market optimists, not pessimists. 'Government is not the solution to our problem; government is the problem . . . It is time to check and reverse the growth of government.' So said

Reagan in his inaugural address. Reagan's tax cuts were intended to be permanent, not counter-cyclical – part of a new agenda for cutting down the state. As soon as Reagan reached the White House he started receiving intelligence briefings which showed that 'Communism as we knew it was approaching the brink of collapse . . . The Soviet economy was . . . a basket case, partly because of massive spending on armaments . . . there were rumblings of nationalist fervor within the captive Soviet empire . . . I wondered how we as a nation could use these cracks in the Soviet system to accelerate the process of collapse.'[10] For the first time, Western leaders sensed that time was running out for Soviet Communism. 'I believe', Reagan said in his 'evil empire' speech of 8 March 1983, 'that . . . [the] last pages [of Communism] even now are being written'.

When Mikhail Gorbachev became general secretary of the Communist Party of the Soviet Union in 1985, he, too, faced an entirely different world from that which had confronted Nikita Khrushchev thirty years before. Now it was a question not of burying the West, but of saving Communism. The Soviet Union had fallen disastrously behind the West not only in its ability to raise living standards, but, perhaps more importantly from the standpoint of its leadership, in its technology, on which depended its ability to reproduce its military power. Gorbachev's initial reforms seemed to hark back to Khrushchev's, as Reagan's had to Kennedy's. The cycle of liberalization followed by repression had been seen many times already in the Soviet Union's history. But whereas Khrushchev's de-Stalinization of the 1950s was started from a position of economic and ideological confidence, Gorbachev's attempt to de-Brezhnevize the Soviet economy started from a position of economic and ideological exhaustion. Political belief had all but drained out of the system. Living conditions, never good, had started to deteriorate. Gorbachev knew that capitalism could no longer be taken 'from the rear'. That is why the reassertion of central control in response to American rearmament was never a realistic option.

Reagan's aim was to get the Soviets to 'sue for peace'.[11] On

15 January 1986 they did just that. In a public letter to Reagan, Gorbachev called for nuclear disarmament. He made it clear that he wanted to extricate the Soviet Union from Afghanistan. Implicitly, he acknowledged that the dream of world Communism was over. At the Reykjavik summit of October 1986, Gorbachev agreed to massive reductions in Soviet nuclear and conventional forces. In 1988 he told the United Nations, 'Our ideal is a world community of states with political systems and foreign policies based on law.' Even so, the speed of Communism's collapse took all observers by surprise. At the beginning of 1989 the 'evil empire' was still intact, if tottering; by 1991 it was all over.

By accident rather than design, the United States, it seemed, had brought about the defeat of Communism on the terms it wanted. By keeping up the military pressure, it had prolonged the life of the party-state dictatorship to the point at which it could no longer reproduce itself and had ceased to inspire anyone else. This achievement was bought at a high cost. The ideological obsession of the United States not only destroyed Soviet Communism but damaged Western economies. Permanent macroeconomic imbalance was the price it paid for the defeat of Communism. That is why the victory of freedom has left such a disturbing legacy of economic and political problems. But, in truth, there was no other way. It was the very simplicity of the American ideology which enabled it to outlast the sophistries of Marxism-Leninism, and the sophistication of the West's intellectual élites, in remarkable affirmation of Hegel's cunning of reason.

The rise and fall of Communism is part of the larger story of how the world tasted the fruit and came to reject the temptation of collectivism. The shape of the world after Communism will be largely determined by how well we understand, and respond to, this larger movement of history.

CHAPTER TWO

THE NATURE OF COLLECTIVISM

The great ideological struggle of the twentieth century has been between collectivism and liberalism.* Collectivism was defined eighty years ago by the English jurist Albert Dicey as 'government for the good of the people by experts or officials who know or think they know what is good for the people better than any non-official person or than the mass of the people themselves'.[1] The economist Friedrich Hayek was to define it in 1944 as 'the deliberate organization of the labours of society for a definite social goal'.[2] The centralized planning of a society's future seems to be the essential feature of collectivism: a collectivist society is one in which state purposes have replaced private purposes in shaping economic and social life. As the former Labour Cabinet minister Douglas Jay is supposed to have said, 'The gentleman in Whitehall knows best.' The possibility of collectivism resulted directly from the enhanced organizational and economic capacity of the modern state. It is this feature which distinguishes collectivism from all previous interferences of rulers with the lives of their subjects.

Where is collectivism to be placed on the traditional Left – Right axis of modern politics? Historically, it is associated with the rise of socialism, with its belief in social justice, or equality, as an end, and public ownership, planning and spending as means. Certainly there was always a very strong socialist flavour

---

* Throughout the book I use 'liberalism' in its nineteenth-century European sense. In the United States, 'liberalism' came to stand for socialism, or social democracy, partly because the New Deal liberals were about as far to the Left as mainstream American politics went. For the American reader, by 'liberalism' I mean 'conservatism', the doctrine of limited government.

about collectivism, because socialists, above all, wanted to achieve results which were not guaranteed, or which were positively prevented, by the market system, or by the existing power system, or by the interaction of both. But throughout this century there have been non-socialist forms, distinguished from socialism by different aims, such as the promotion of economic growth or the building up of national power. In practice, it became increasingly difficult to distinguish socialism from varieties of national socialism, or collectivist nationalism. Socialists used to stand distinctively for state ownership of industry, but as the twentieth century wore on they came to place less emphasis on this aspect, more on central planning and public spending. Conversely, Fascism and its many imitators in developing countries have used state ownership selectively.

It is better to keep purpose out of it, and to think of collectivism as an ideologically neutral technique of non-market coordination of economic life for the purpose of achieving whatever it is that the collectivist wants to achieve. In this technical sense, collectivism was invented in the First World War, although the collectivist mood dates from earlier. As a planning technique, it could be used by the Left, the Right or anyone. Socialists would always claim that their brand of collectivism was superior to that of any other, as being directed to nobler ends and rooted in a much wider base of support. Whether or not this is true – and it must be remembered that Hitler, who called himself a 'National Socialist', got more popular support in Germany than any Communist Party has achieved in free elections – from the liberal point of view it is the technique of coordination and control, with its explicit or implicit assumption that the centre knows best, which is the salient and objectionable feature of collectivism. That is why liberal political science has invented a single name – totalitarianism – for collectivist organization carried to extremes, whatever its ostensible purpose. However, the identification of collectivism with totalitarianism fails to identify intermediate, partial and certainly more humane expressions of the same tendency which nevertheless rest on the same central assumption that reason is located at the centre.

Collectivism is conventionally contrasted with classic liberalism or individualism – with a model of a society whose labours are coordinated through the market system, and in which social outcomes are the unplanned sum of private choices. The claim to central control is based on the claim to centralized knowledge; whereas the liberal argument for spontaneous coordination rests on the primary value attached to liberty and on the existence of dispersed knowledge which cannot be centralized. In a collectivist society the state enlists the law to serve its aims; in a liberal society the law sets limits to what a state can do.

The identification of liberalism with individualism, while polemically useful, is conceptually flawed. Nineteenth-century liberalism had two aims which partly conflicted. The first was to release the individual from social fetters; the second was to disperse power. The first was directed against the tyranny of custom; the second against monarchical and all other forms of despotism. Both the recognition of an inviolable private sphere and the recognition that the public sphere should not be dominated by state monopoly are inseparable from what we mean by liberalism; but they are not the same.

The French Revolution attacked feudalism in the name of individual rights, and attacked royal despotism in the name of a feudal order of dispersed power. The politics of post-Revolutionary Europe flowed from this division. The idea of a state created by contract and the project of a market economy best expressed the individualist thrust of liberalism. Modern conservatism, by contrast, largely flows from liberalism's decentralizing aim.[3] Its social vision was of an updated medievalism, in which individual rights against the sovereign were embedded in a mass of involuntary and voluntary associations. For liberal-conservatives like Tocqueville, the decisive barrier to despotism was thus not unfettered individualism but the existence of a moral order capable of withstanding the encroachment of the state.* In democracies, Tocqueville said, 'all become powerless if they do not learn to help one another voluntarily'.[4] The habit of association in turn invests self-interest with a degree of publicness. Both liberals and conservatives have supported the competitive market system. But whereas liberals typically wish to extend it for the sake of individual liberty, conservatives typically wish to limit it for the sake of preserving tradition. Many conservatives as well as socialists have regarded the unrestrained expansion of the market as atomizing society, thus paving the way for collectivism.

Classical liberals have always recognized an important role for the state, and do not think of all state activities as necessarily collectivist in aim or practice. To have a government, even a strong and active government, does not make a society collectivist. Private arrangements cannot provide societies with all the goods and services which people want. That is why we have states. States may be regarded as existing to fill the inevitable gaps in the protective and regulatory mechanisms of civil society – gaps which economists anaesthetize in the phrase 'market failure' – though people have argued about how large these gaps are and where they are located. Classical liberals typically think of society as a traffic system, in which the state promulgates and enforces the rules of the road and provides a breakdown service, without which no safe traffic can take place. Collectivism enters at the point when the state seeks to direct the flow of traffic towards particular ends, or for the benefit of particular groups.

There are four grey areas between collectivism and noncollectivism which in practice make it difficult to distinguish between state activity which supports a liberal society and state activity which undermines it. The first is regulation. Regulation is part of the government's basic function of protecting people from harms – for example, through food standards, licensing

---

* Conservatives recognized that individual premises could lead to collectivist conclusions if, as in utilitarianism, traditions were seen as obstacles to creating the conditions of maximum happiness.

laws, etc. The quantity of regulation tends to grow over time, as society becomes more urbanized, and as people's conception of harm is enlarged. (The law would not have intervened in the past to protect animals or the environment against people.) Regulation can produce a collectivist drift if the concept of harm is extended unduly: beyond a certain point the 'nanny' state and the collectivist state become indistinguishable. Regulation is a potent source of collectivist creep. It is associated with bureaucracy and administrative law. It is perhaps the characteristic form of collectivism in the United States. Another potent contemporary source of regulation is the Brussels bureaucracy. All societies which want to stay free should have regular bonfires of accumulated regulations.

The second grey area arises from the existence of mixed public goods. In principle, public-goods theory is merely a more rigorous restatement of the social-contract ideas of liberal political philosophers. Peaceful coexistence in a state of nature is impossible, because protection cannot be guaranteed by private contract. So it is rational for individuals to enter into a 'social contract' by which they renounce their right to self-defence in return for the protection of a sovereign. Security of life and property is thus the primary 'public good' which brings forth the state and which defines (and in Locke's view limits) its powers.

The main technical characteristics of public goods are that they cannot be supplied in individual amounts and people cannot be excluded from using them. A national defence system cannot be tailored to suit individual requirements, and no one can be deprived of its benefits. Given these characteristics, public goods cannot be marketed: the rational consumer would understate his demand for them, in the hope of getting other people to pay the cost of the benefit he hoped to enjoy – what economists call 'free-riding'. Voluntary contributions will not pay the cost of providing an adequate street-lighting system in towns, because of the free-rider problem. But no one will refuse taxes to pay for street-lighting. The state is set up to provide public goods through compulsory contributions. Thus public-goods theory gives an elegant explanation of the social contract.

A practical conclusion follows: wherever free-riding is possible, there is a case for taxation. The problem is that, apart from 'pure' public goods like defence and law and order, there are 'mixed' goods like health care and education which provide both individual and shared benefits. The benefit to society of having an educated population may be more than the sum of the individual benefits to its members from being educated. The shared benefits and harms of mixed goods are called 'externalities'. The prediction is that the market will undersupply the shared benefits. Conversely, it is likely to oversupply such 'bad' externalities as pollution, because firms do not have to 'cost' pollution unless they are made to. Cigarette-smoking is said to cause shared as well as private harms; an excise tax on cigarettes can be justified in terms of making smokers pay for the harm they inflict on others by smoking. The trouble is that, in the hands of anyone with sufficient desire to interfere in people's lives, the doctrine of shared benefits and harms can give the state almost unlimited warrant to forbid, regulate or reshape private activities.

A third grey area is created by the theory of democracy, especially in its modern form of the democratic mandate. In the nineteenth century democracy was generally seen as a support for limited government, largely because the franchise was controlled by the minority of property owners. With the extension of democracy to the propertyless (a step resisted by John Stuart Mill), democracy came to be seen as an instrument for improving the position of the poor through the political process – by, for example, using the tax system to redistribute wealth. The question then was how this could be reconciled with an original social contract designed to protect the rights of lawfully acquired property. This battle has been fought out over the extent and purposes of the welfare state. The underlying division has been between the 'reluctant collectivists' whose welfare objective was to establish a 'social safety net', made necessary by failures in the private markets for insurance, and the egalitarians who wanted to use the tax system to transfer wealth and income from the rich to the poor.[5] In practice, all state welfare systems have combined elements of both 'insurance' and 're-distribution' – i.e. they have had some collectivist intent. A re-distributive motive implies a much larger 'transfer' role for the state than does an 'insurance' one.

But the pathologies of democracy do not stop here. A majoritarian public-choice rule implies the right of a majority, however small, to coerce the minority – something which liberals would oppose. Thus the democratic mandate can be used to justify transfers of income from minorities to majorities. It can also be a cover for the 'capture' of governments by powerful producer interests who can divert income flows to themselves. In the absence of what Hayek calls a 'constitution of liberty', the doctrine of the democratic mandate offers no obstacle to a persisting collectivist encroachment on the sphere of spontaneous action, and may easily sanction it.

Perhaps the most problematic grey area of all is summed up in the elusive idea of 'corporatism'. Liberal theory is consistent with a rich variety of collective associations – even those given statutory rights of self-regulation of professional standards. Indeed, the existence of such 'intermediate' groups is a source of vitality, not decay, for liberal societies. It is a different matter when governments create private monopolies as agents of policy – more formally, grant groups 'certain institutionalized or *ad hoc* benefits in return for guarantees by the groups' representatives that their members will behave in certain ways considered to be in the public interest'.[6] Corporatism can be defined as a form of non-market, non-bureaucratic coordination – a way of pressing pluralism into the service of the state. Its strongest expression was in Italian Fascism, but corporatist arrangements have been widespread in democracies. For example, democratic governments have promoted centralized industrial bargaining in an effort to achieve income control or growth targets. The criticism of corporatist arrangements is that they confer privilege without clear accountability.[7] In essence they are attempts to get functional groups to police state policy. They typically come into play when the state's reach has come to exceed its grasp – when both state authority and the market system are failing. If such 'vested' interests deliver the coordination the government wants, they cease to fulfil their democratic function of protecting society from the state; if, like Frankenstein's monster, they escape from their inventor's control, they make the market economy unworkable without delivering coordination. That is why corporatism is best seen as an unstable halfway house with a tendency to move on to full-blooded collectivism or to collapse back into market economy. This is relevant to the fate of Western corporatism in the 1970s.

Collectivism is therefore a matter of degree. When we talk of 'the collectivist age' we are talking both about the degree of direction of social life and about the trend for the function and activities of the state to expand. It is a matter of great importance in political theory, and indeed to human happiness, whether the state pursues its aims humanely or by methods of terror, by manipulating prices or by prohibiting choice, but this does not affect the definition of collectivism. What it means is that collectivism is compatible with a large variety of political and economic constitutions, though not all.

The degree of collectivism in any given society is roughly measurable, though I am not aware of any attempt to construct a 'collectivism index'. One can use a number of different measures. All of them show that over the course of this century collectivism has increased – often dramatically. The most important measure is the fraction of output a government spends. In 1880 the average of public spending as a share of GNP in six selected industrial countries was 10 per cent. By 1985 it had reached 47 per cent. This increase had included a large rise in the ratio of public to private investment – from near zero to an average of 30 per cent in industrial countries over the last hundred years. In the Communist countries these two ratios have typically been close to 100 per cent. The public spending/GNP ratio is *the* crucial measure of collectivism, because the larger the share of the national income which the state spends, the greater its ability to determine what is produced. That is why

Adam Smith insisted that revenue should be raised only for the state's necessary functions – defence, law and order, and the provision of public goods needed to 'facilitate commerce in general'.

Another measure of collectivism is the fraction of output produced by the state. Over the collectivist era the share of output produced by firms and services owned by the state has grown enormously. In the Communist countries the proportion typically reached over 90 per cent; in the developed capitalist countries it had grown from near zero in 1900 to 20 per cent by the 1970s. In many capitalist countries such 'commanding heights' of the economy as transportation (roads, railways, buses, airlines, dockyards, shipbuilding), energy (gas, electricity, water, coal, oil), communications (post office, telephones, radio and television) and 'essential industries' (steel, motor cars) came to be publicly owned, mainly as the result of post-1945 nationalizations; in addition, state provision of services such as education, health care and housing grew enormously relative to private provision. As a result, the proportion of state employees in the workforce also rose dramatically – in Britain, for example, from 2.4 per cent in 1850 to 29.6 per cent in 1978. The larger the size of the state-owned sector of the economy, the more the state will be able to ensure that only what it wants is produced. In a state-owned economy, influence through purchase is replaced by direct control of production.

A third crude indicator of collectivism is the amount of interference with cross-border flows of goods, capital and labour. This typically includes tariffs, quotas, subsidies and other non-tariff barriers; exchange controls; restrictions on migration. Such interference may be thought of as measuring the degree of autarky or self-sufficiency. For example, in 1975 18.4 per cent of the British government's budget went into subsidies to the public and private sectors of the economy, again representing a growth from zero before the First World War.

The progressiveness of the tax system may be taken as a fourth measure – the degree of progression measuring the state's redistributive intent. Finally, we may try to measure the extent of regulation, as, for example, in the growth in the number of regulatory agencies.

The issue here is not whether state taxation and spending policies, or public ownership of industry, or regulation, create a society more or less efficient or just than it would have been in the absence of such features. It is that they create a society which is different from what it would have been. Herein lies the chief flaw of collectivism. It is that, outside exceptional periods, the degree of consent for the reshaping of the economy and society is always more limited than the ambitions of the collectivists. This becomes increasingly obvious as the results of the reshaping become apparent. Beyond a certain point, the expansion of state activities produces its own specific pathologies – the piling up of unwanted production, the emergence of a pattern of income distribution which undermines incentives to wealth creation and self-improvement, the spread of the 'dictatorship of the official', the proliferation of corporatist arrangements, and above all, widespread corruption and 'rent-seeking'. In free countries the lack of consent for these outcomes is manifested in tax revolts, capital flight and election of parties pledged to 'roll back the state'. In Communist countries, where such 'spontaneous' actions are forbidden, resentment builds up till the regime itself is overthrown. Hayek argued in 1944 that 'once the communal sector . . . exceeds a certain proportion of the whole, the effects of its action dominate the whole system'.[8]

The trend of political economy in the twentieth century may be summed up as follows. The tremendous increase in the political, administrative, and organizational capacity of the modern state, together with its power of economic calculation, has tempted it to do too much. As the performance of states worsened, so the resistance to their pretensions grew, forcing a retreat from collectivism back to market economy. This is the meaning of the transition through which we are living.

CHAPTER THREE

THE RISE OF COLLECTIVISM

Since collectivism in practice has been so various, its essential character is best conveyed by contrast with what preceded it. 'Until August 1914', wrote A. J. P. Taylor, 'a sensible, law-abiding Englishman could pass through life and hardly notice the existence of the state, beyond the post office and the policeman.' This, he went on to say, was changed by the First World War. 'The mass of the people became, for the first time, active citizens. Their lives were shaped by orders from above; they were required to serve the state instead of pursuing exclusively their own affairs . . . The state established a hold over its citizens which, though relaxed in peacetime, was never again to be removed and which the Second World War was again to increase.'[1]

The contrast between before and after is too extreme; the notion of the First World War as the catalyst too dramatic. Nevertheless, it is true that the extensive role of the state in shaping twentieth-century economic life reversed the nineteenth-century trend to non-interference in the production and distribution of wealth. Some aspects, at least, of the modern state's role seem to hark back to earlier times when the wealth of subjects and foreigners alike was considered fit for rulers to command at will, for their greater power, splendour, and prestige.

These earlier economies were what Sir John Hicks called 'tribute' or 'revenue' economies – support systems for the ruler and his servants. Market economies grew up on the edges of revenue economies, and eventually market relations between subjects replaced tributary relations between subjects and sovereigns. In the twentieth century there has been a 'massive

swingback towards the Revenue Economy', though one 'profoundly transformed by experience of market forces.'[2] The return of the revenue economy came after a century in which
market forces had enormously expanded the wealth and productive powers of the leading countries. The state's claim to
revenue had to be justified, therefore, by the promise that the
state's revenue would be used to increase wealth and welfare
beyond what market forces could achieve. Soviet Communism,
the most complete twentieth-century expression of the revenue
economy, claimed that central planning of a publicly owned
economy would allocate resources more efficiently, cause them
to grow faster, and distribute them more justly than could a
privately owned market economy. The question has always
been whether collectivism is a genuinely new form of economic
organization, or merely the old predatory state decked out in
the specious garments of rationality. Twentieth-century experience has given some answer to this question.

From the early eighteenth century it was apparent that a few
countries in Western European, notably England and Holland,
had started to pull away from the stagnant empires of the Ori-
ent in both wealth and power. Modern economics started as an
attempt to explain why. Using the *a prioristic* method, which
subsequently became the hallmark of economics, Adam Smith
argued, in his *Wealth of Nations* (1776), that the source of economic growth lay in people's 'natural propensity to truck, barter and exchange'. By promoting the division of labour and the
accumulation of stock, trade increased not just the wealth but
the 'productive powers' of all engaging in it. State policy could
promote or hinder wealth-creation. Drawing from British experience, he argued that the wealth of nations grows faster if
the state refrains from taxing, regulating, or directing commerce, but confines itself to providing the conditions of 'natural
liberty' in which private commerce can prosper. The 'English
ideology' was rounded off with the claim that free trade promoted peace, since it benefited all participants.

The German economist Friedrich List drew the opposite

conclusion from the facts of England's rise to commercial supremacy. In his *National System of Political Economy* (1844), he claimed that England had industrialized under Protection and used naval power and unequal treaties to force its exports on others. England now aimed to protect its industrial monopoly by preaching free trade, like the climber who throws away the ladder by which he has reached the top. The German states should follow what England had practised, not what it preached, by creating a customs union stretching from the 'mouth of the Rhine to the frontier of Poland', behind whose tariff barriers they could industrialize too. List wrote: 'If, therefore, a sacrifice of *value* is caused by protective duties, it is made good by the gain of a *power of production*, which not only secures to the nation an infinitely greater amount of material resources, but also industrial independence in case of war.'[3] This argument for protecting 'infant industries' neatly combined the new concern for wealth-creation with the older promotion of national power. The 'English' and 'German' ideologies have competed for mastery in the twentieth century. List is the father of 'development economics'. It is the state's duty to foster the growth of manufactures so that poor states can catch up with rich ones. Its claim to tax the consumer for the benefit of the producer marks the first point for the re-entry of the 'revenue economy'.

The second re-entry point was Marxism. In the *Communist Manifesto*, which appeared four years after List's *National Economy*, Karl Marx claimed that capitalist accumulation took place by depriving workers of the fruits of their labour, having first deprived them of their customary property holdings, which left them nothing to sell but their 'labour power'. In this unjust investment mechanism lay the doom of the system. An enlarging supply of capital goods would reduce the profit rate without expanding the purchasing power of the masses. The only solution was for the revolutionary state to 'expropriate the expropriators' and share out the fruits of progress; or, in the social democratic version, to redistribute the stolen surplus through progressive taxation. The exploitation doctrine became the charter myth of the trade unions and socialist parties which were formed in the late nineteenth century to 'reclaim' the unpaid portion of working-class toil.

Economic nationalism was about growth, Marxism about redistribution. But both, by taking as their starting point an initial act of spoliation, and treating economic liberalism as an ideological device to maintain advantages unfairly gained, showed they were really in the business of redistributing wealth and power from the haves to the have-nots, whether the haves were states or classes. Twentieth-century Marxism-Leninism would combine both approaches in an explosive mixture.

The shift from individualism to collectivism at the end of the nineteenth century was precipitated by a change in economic and social facts which helped convince people that progress could no longer be safely entrusted to spontaneous activity. As we have seen, the notion of dispersal was central to the liberal project – the dispersal of all kinds of power over resources and ideas. Economic power would be spread among many small independent producers (typically family firms), none of whom would be in a position to corner the market; population would be dispersed in small or medium-sized towns set in largely rural communities; political power would be dispersed domestically through the abolition of aristocratic privileges, an enlarged franchise, and constitutional arrangements, and internationally through the replacement of existing dynastic empires by self-governing nation-states. Social protection would be entrusted to a 'moral economy' of families, neighbourhoods, philanthropic bodies, mutual assurance associations. It was a premise of liberal economics that business fluctuations would become less intense as countries adopted sound banking and free-trade practices, and that wars would disappear with the hegemony of a pacific business class. Mid-nineteenth-century facts conformed to this picture sufficiently to recommend it as a general model of progress, dependent only on the spread of liberal economic and political mechanisms to backward areas.

However, the dominant facts which seized the imagination at the end of the century all had to do with concentration: the concentration of capital in big business; the concentration of labour in big trade unions; the concentration of population in huge cities; the division of politics into class parties; the division of the world into competing empires. These developments were associated, as both cause and effect, with the growing amplitude of the business cycle: the years 1873–1896 saw the first modern 'world depression'. The integration of the world market on the basis of competitive agriculture and industry led to a succession of crises of overcapacity, with collapses in prices and profits; the crises in turn promoted further concentration of industry and distribution by eliminating the 'inefficient' small manufacturer and trader. The needs of large-scale organization seemed to dictate a bureaucratic pattern of coordination which undermined the market as the main locus of spontaneous agency.

The 'new fact' which most alarmed, but also impressed, contemporaries was the changing nature of business organization. In a number of sectors, processes of production and distribution hitherto carried out in a competitive market of small owner-controlled firms now became part of the 'internalized' operations of large corporations. In the United States especially, the corporation came to be seen as a self-contained planning system, integrating supplies, production, marketing and distribution within a single organization; run by large staffs of professional managers and experts arranged in a hierarchy; equipped with assembly-line production and the latest principles of 'scientific management' (Taylorism); and controlling its own prices. The modern business corporation was seen both as a threat (in its private form) and as a model (if 'socialized') for the whole economic and social system. 'By crushing out of existence the . . . economically unfit . . . the great commercial and industrial concerns of to-day are paving the way to their own absorption by the community; and by rendering it possible for the man of small means, but of ability . . . to direct a vast undertaking, they have shown how it is possible to train officials to conduct vast organizations for a remuneration the merest fraction of which went to the former "captain of industry".' So wrote one ardent collectivist in 1914.[4] Another remarked, 'The perfect form of the trust is the state.'⁵ The argument was that, with the inevitable supersession of market capitalism by organized capitalism, private bureaucracies pursuing private purposes had to be coordinated by a national bureaucracy pursuing public purposes.

Another fact which alarmed contemporaries was the changing character of international exchange. Competitive trade was replacing complementary trade in agriculture and manufacturing, while growing capital exports from the rich countries were integrating the world into a network of creditors and debtors. Competition bred protective business and labour organization, which made economies less flexible; foreign capital penetration excited the latent forces of radical nationalism. 'To expect that a community would remain indifferent to the scourge of unemployment, the shifting of industries and occupations and to the moral and psychological torture accompanying them, merely because the economic effects, in the long run, might be beneficial, was to assume an absurdity,' wrote Karl Polanyi.⁶ The British statesman Joseph Chamberlain ironically expressed the same idea in his campaign for tariff reform in 1903: 'Look how easy it is. Your once great trade in sugar refining is gone; all right, try jam. Your iron trade is going; never mind, you can make mousetraps. The cotton trade is threatened; well, what does that matter to you? Suppose you try dolls' eyes . . . But how long is this to go on?' The British feared that foreign manufactures were robbing them of their markets; foreigners feared that British capital was robbing them of their independence. States could no longer be indifferent to the flow of trade and money, impinging as it did on relative national power.

The growth of parallel organizations of labour engaging with organized capital in increasingly costly and disruptive industrial struggles suggested the need for a new principle of social integration, or reintegration. Nationalism, socialism, corporatism and imperialism all offered themselves as solutions to the class war. Broadly speaking, the nationalists and imperialists wanted to dissolve class into nation, and the socialists to dissolve nation into class. A new generation of liberals talked of the need to create harmonizing, reconciling institutions, of 'social justice' between the classes. All rejected *laissez-faire* attitudes to production and distribution.

A further alarming fact was the 'closing of the frontier' – the exhaustion of North America's 'public domain' of free land which had accommodated successive waves of westward-moving immigrant farmers from Europe. The American historian of the frontier Frederick Jackson Pollock saw the availability of land as the 'dominant force in creating a democracy and making the individual free from Old World restrictions'. With the 'frontier of opportunity' gone, 'discontent is demanding an extension of governmental activity on its behalf'. The declining availability of free land confined the still rapidly growing populations of European stock to a predominantly urban existence. Huge cities grew up on well-tried principles of private philanthropy and *laissez-faire*, but, unlike small communities, they could not be run by spontaneous social regulation. Their requirements for sanitation, health, education, transport, heating, lighting and other utilities and amenities could be met only by 'municipal socialism'. Urbanization also drew attention to the problem of 'poverty in the midst of plenty', largely hidden in the countryside, or accepted as a 'fact of life'. The enfranchisement of the urban masses brought 'social demands' into the centre of politics, articulated by new model political parties of Right and Left which gradually replaced the parliamentary middle-class liberal parties wedded to non-interference. Governments started to provide 'social safety nets' for the old, sick and unemployed. The willingness of the rich to pay for them testifies not just to the fear of social disorder but also to the growth of a middle-class social conscience, stimulated by the revelations of urban poverty.

However, it would be a mistake to assume that the growth of collectivism was in any simple way a response to 'new facts' or 'new imperatives'. That state responsibility needed to expand is indisputable. 'Modernization' enlarged, exposed or *created* 'gaps' in inherited systems of social self-regulation which the state was bound to fill. Gaps in the provision of education and insurance are classic examples; the adulteration of food is another. Problems of this kind led to the emergence of an undogmatic kind of welfarism, particularly in Germany and Britain. But the collectivist temper was not centrally a product of this kind of problem: it was the perceived growth in the ability of private capital to disrupt the social order and the international ranking of states which created the collectivist mood.

It has been noted often enough, though frequently forgotten, that late-nineteenth-century collectivism was post-Marxist, acquiring a Marxist component only because of Marxism's extraordinary ability to mutate into new shapes. Classic Marxism was an outgrowth of classical liberalism; its 'problematic' had nothing to do with big business as such. What it was concerned to deny was that free trade – or more generally a capitalist market economy – created a harmony of interests between capitalists and workers. It was a product, that is, of the wrenching effects of the first Industrial Revolution. By the time the *Communist Manifesto* appeared, in 1848, Marxism, in its reliance on the labour theory of value, was already technically obsolete. Basing himself on this theory, Marx was able to demonstrate fairly rigorously that any firm which covered its costs – including the cost of capital – was exploiting the worker: since capital was only embodied labour power, the surplus over the price of labour which accrued to the owner of capital as profit was simply a subtraction from the worker's share. Much more interesting than this piece of scholasticism was Marx's vision of the evolution of the capitalist system based on it. He foresaw that increasing competition and the tendency of wages to encroach on profits would produce periodic crises of profitability, leading to a growing concentration of capital in the hands of fewer owners. Thus what Marxists called 'monopolization' was endogenous to the capitalist 'accumulation' process. Continuous capital-deepening – increasing the ratio of machines to labour – was essential to create and replenish a reserve army of the unemployed to keep wages down to subsistence, leading to the polarization of industry between an ever smaller class of owners and an ever larger class of 'wage slaves'. These measures would not solve the crisis of profitability, because labour is the only source of capitalist 'accumulation', but, by removing all the intermediate forms of private property, they would clear the ground for the final confrontation between a proletarianized society and the remaining big capitalists. It has often been wondered why Marx failed to take into account technical progress, which would have made it possible to pay the worker more while maintaining the ratio of profits to wages. The answer is that there is no technical progress in his system, merely the application of increasing quantities of the machines to production. One of the extraordinary ironies of history is that this was precisely the method used by the Soviet authorities to promote the economic development of their societies. The Marxist prophecy of stagnating living standards came true only under Communism.

Marxism was rescued from obsolescence by two developments, and by one superb piece of ideological invention. By the end of the nineteenth century there were tendencies to monopoly in certain sectors of all industrial and industrializing economies, and particularly in two countries – the United States and Germany. Under pure monopoly conditions – where there is only one firm producing a product and many buyers – exploitation of the worker in Marx's sense becomes possible – that is, the firm can earn above-normal profits. Thus the growth of private monopoly became an argument for public ownership to stop firms exploiting the worker. (Economists were also turning up examples of 'natural' monopolies like gas, electricity and water distribution where competition is wasteful.) Secondly, and contrary to the expectations of the classical liberals, business cycles were becoming deeper and more long-lasting, saddling capitalism with the wastefulness and misery of unemployment. Clearly, the invisible hand was proving to be something of a broken reed. Popular explanations of business oscillations had little connection with Marx's theory of crises, itself difficult enough to understand. One popular theory was that a group of financiers sat in Wall Street or London, deflating the currency in order to bankrupt debtors, and then inflating it to make huge profits out of the property they had impounded. Still, the oscillations of the economy reinforced Marx's picture of a system lurching aimlessly from crisis to crisis.

The Achilles' heel of the Marxist prophecy of growing immiseration was the observed fact that workers' wages were rising. This, as one would expect, was due to technical progress, the factor left out of Marx's theory. Socialist parties attributed it to trade-union pressure, and drew the conclusion that revolution was unnecessary. Lenin struck back with a brilliant invention. Firms in the capital 'core' were able to bribe their workers with the 'super-profits' of imperialism! Even as the rate of exploitation was falling in the developed world, it was being increased by incorporating the underdeveloped peripheries of Europe into a competitive system of world monopoly capitalism (imperialism). But this only delayed the end, since the enlarged system was subject to exactly the same contradictions as before. The case for revolution was unchanged, but an international dimension had been added to the class struggle. Thus was Marxism relaunched as Marxism-Leninism.[7] In the twentieth century this was to become one of the charter myths of the poor nations, with the Soviet Union and China standing as the great exemplars of how to break out of the circle of exploitation.

There is undoubted power in Lenin's update of classical Marxism. Although its economic theory was no better than the original, it captured one important feature of contemporary reality: the growing interpenetration of business and politics. There seemed to be a nexus uniting big business and state policy which undermined the classical liberal theory of the separation of state and market, and which seemed to be involved in the new imperialism in Africa and the growing rivalry of nations. Thus Lenin saw imperialism as the 'monopoly stage' of capitalism, with industrial/banking trusts locked into a global struggle for profits which was bound to lead to wars for the 'division and redivision of the world' between the great capitalist monopolies.

Lenin saw the state as the agent of big business – or rather he failed to recognize any relevant distinction between the two. This was to have a baleful effect on the conduct of Soviet foreign policy after the Bolshevik Revolution. When Nikolai Novikov, the Soviet ambassador to America, cabled home in 1946 that the need of European and Asian countries for goods which only 'American monopolistic capitalism' could supply would 'be a stage on the road to world domination by the United States', he was merely echoing the Leninist doctrine that the state *was* monopoly capitalism.[8]

However, the nexus between big business and politics could be explained in another way, which on the whole made more sense. This was that many states deliberately created and used big business for the purpose of state- or nation-building. Sergei Witte, the Russian finance minister, used this argument in 1900 to persuade the tsar that state-financed industrialization was a vital *political* necessity: 'If we do not take energetic and decisive measures . . . then the rapidly growing foreign industries will break through our tariff barriers and establish themselves in our fatherland . . . and drive their roots into the depths of our economy. This may gradually clear the way also for triumphant political penetration by foreign powers . . . Our economic backwardness may lead to political and cultural backwardness as well.'[9] (Conversely, the French government was encouraging the investment of the savings of the French peasant in Russian government bonds to strengthen the Franco-Russian alliance.) 'Monopoly capitalism' could never have achieved the privileged position it came to occupy in the political and economic life of Central and Eastern Europe before 1914 without state protection. Lenin deliberately obscured the distinction between, on the one hand, the transmuting of feudal privileges into industrial monopolies to serve the power aims of the dynastic state and, on the other, the capitalistic development of large-scale enterprise in response to technological innovation and market demand.

In its Leninist form, Marxism proved highly compatible with economic nationalism. In making the case for the protection of 'infant industries', List used a modern-sounding argument: industry, unlike agriculture, was subject to increasing returns to scale.

But soon an argument appeared for protecting agriculture as well. The transport and refrigeration revolution made possible the widescale import of food from areas where land was cheap to areas where it was expensive. This caused a collapse in food prices in the 1870s. The German economist Adolph Wagner claimed that it was against the interests of the state to allow industrialization to go too far: tariffs should be imposed on agricultural imports, to retain a due balance among the branches of the national economy. The two forms of protectionism were combined in Bismarck's 'iron and rye' tariff of 1879, which meant that Germany's pre-war consumers paid food prices between 50 per cent and 300 per cent higher than abroad. The same could be said for the modern European consumer.

The doctrine of economic nationalism linked political nationalism to protectionism rather than to free trade. This link was ominous for two reasons. First, it weakened the power of trade to pacify nationalism. Secondly, the domestic markets created for the products of protected heavy industries largely consisted of state procurements for military purposes. Thus protectionist policies driven by nationalist resentment at inferior status automatically created 'military-industrial complexes' dependent on state orders which, by igniting arms races, increased general insecurity, requiring higher tariffs, more militarization, etc. This was the seed-bed of twentieth-century collectivism.

One of the grosser misreadings by late-nineteenth-century thinkers was their confusion between monopoly and bigness. The growth in the average size of firms does not necessarily mean a reduction in competition, or even in the number of firms. Firms were growing larger – but so were markets. The arrival of the large business corporation can be largely explained by new cost-reducing technologies of production, transport and communications. 'The age of coal and iron', wrote the historian Geoffrey Barraclough, 'was succeeded, after 1870, by the age of steel and electricity, of oil and chemicals.'[10] Older manufacturing operations could be carried out by small firms, with small capitals, but the new technology could be embodied in production only by much bigger firms producing on a much larger scale. This was because the capital outlays needed to install the new technology could be mobilized only by large units, and be justified only by large and continuous production runs. The new technology created a much more integrated world market as 'Industry . . . went out into the world in search of the basic materials without which, in its newest forms, it could not exist.'[11] Given the big capital outlays required for the development of raw-material production, much of this integration took the form of foreign (European and North American) ownership and control of the agriculture, mining, oil-production, utilities and distribution sectors in Latin America, the Middle East and East Asia. Because of the welfare gains from this kind of integration, it is basically an optimistic story, unless seen through nationalist or Marxist spectacles, as it tended to be in Latin America.

The liberals made the obvious point that governments had their own agendas, particularly in foreign policy – the domain of princes, diplomats and generals – to which they could attach sections of business largely dependent on state orders. Like all good entrepreneurs, political leaders also set out to create a demand for their favoured projects, aided and abetted by the yellow press. Right-wing parties whipped up nationalism and played on foreign threats to secure increased budgetary allocations for armaments; Left-wing parties played the class-war theme to justify 'soaking the rich'. In the United States, populism mobilized the farmers and small businessmen of middle America against the big financiers of Wall Street. City life bred a mass mind 'hostile to reason, shifty, irritable, credulous and violent',[12] easy prey for conspiracy theories and delusive promises of racist, imperialist or socialist redemption. In both Europe and the United States, nationalism, social reform and imperialism were bundled up in heady political packages.

The ideas by which societies live are supplied by thinkers, though these need not be of high quality. It is facts interpreted by thinkers which determine the way rulers, politicians, businessmen and voters act. These actions in turn affect the reality the thinkers interpret for them. Collectivism was an intellectual construction, a *Zeitgeist*, largely created by a new class of social philosophers, engineers and scientists, often made up of marginal academics, who saw themselves as a rational directing élite 'above class'. The Fabian Society in Britain was a typical example. As Eric Hobsbawm has remarked, 'The Webbs' entire structure of socialism pivots on such professionals. They are the trained, impartial and scientific administrators and expert advisers who have an alternative court of appeal to profit.'[13]

Why a particular intellectual mood caught on at the end of the nineteenth century is difficult to answer, and impossible to answer completely. Many, perhaps most, of the most eminent thinkers of the nineteenth century had never accepted the liberal project (at least in its individualist-economistic form) and what they took to be its fruits – 'the wrenching of work from the protective context of guild, village, and family',[14] the reduction of human relations to what Thomas Carlyle called a 'cash nexus'. With regard to international trade, much European and American thinking remained protectionist, with the tariff seen as an essential support for nation-building. Conservatives turned the individualist argument against itself, pointing out that individualism, by freeing people from their protective associations, left them exposed to the despotic power of the state. Socialists pointed out that market capitalism left workers exposed to the despotic power of the employer. Because it ignored the role of intermediate groups, liberal individualism was vulnerable to attacks of this kind. Growing faith in state action also reflected the more accurate realization that, in an industrial society, economic fluctuations and 'social problems' were not acts of nature to be endured, like harvest failures, but had controllable causes. It also reflected the fact that the state created by the industrial revolution had much greater capacity to deal with these problems. The possibility that governments might not have the knowledge to cure the diseases they were supposed to cure – that they might even be the source of some of them – was a lesson which had to be learnt all over again.

None of these explanations does justice to the degree of pessimism which emerged towards the end of the nineteenth century, a pessimism which contrasted oddly and inexplicably with the triumphs of the machine age and with the exaggerated hopes placed on collective organization. Here again the future as imagined by thinkers cast a long shadow in which societies were destined to walk. The literary intelligentsia rejected industrialization and urbanization in the name of culture. They looked to the state to protect culture against the twin threats of commercialization and democracy, which, as they saw it, would lead to the triumph of greed and ignorance. Fear of the masses powerfully reinforced the tide of cultural pessimism. People were not rational, but easily swayed by unreason, particularly in their social conduct. Once more, liberal thought was indicted: by its neglect of the requirements of social health, it had handed over civilization to financiers, scribblers, mobs. Pessimism infected the public life of all the great nations. Whereas England's ruling class increasingly felt that the meridian of British power had passed, newly arrived, or arriving, nations felt strangled by the Pax Britannica. Europeans as well as Americans were alarmed that the 'closing of the frontier' would doom their populations to the 'unhealthy' life of cities, preventing the dispersion of social tensions and the replenishment of 'healthy' yeomen stocks. They all felt that time was running out for the whites, for beyond the rivalry of the imperial powers stretched the yellow peril, symbolized by Japan's defeat of Russia in the war of 1904–5. Against the multiplying numbers of the non-European races, what resources had the Europeans except their degraded masses of city-dwellers, riven by class conflict?

Here we come as close to the root of *fin-de-siècle* pessimism as we are likely to get. The social thinking of educated people was then much more influenced by history, particularly ancient history, and by science than it is today. A wealthy, urban civilization – so ran the lessons of history – was a civilization in decay. It had lost its religion, its art, its martial qualities – in short, its virtue. It was a civilization of discontented masses in thrall to degenerate plutocrats. Such a civilization was doomed unless it found the means of renewal. Here science came in. Darwinian biology showed that life was a 'struggle for survival'. The new physics, with its reduction of matter to energy, suggested a vitalist theory of leadership, with the human will replacing the old 'laws of progress', whether liberal or Marxist. At bottom the collectivists of Right and Left offered renewal through struggle – a struggle of nations or classes, which would purify and invigorate, would sweep away the degenerate nations or classes, and secure the means of a healthy existence for its victors. For such a struggle, societies had to be organized.

At an abstract level, the two most important replacement ideas for atomistic liberalism were organicism and Hegelianism. The organic superseded the mechanical metaphor: society was more than the sum of its parts. The state or government, far from being a contrivance to guarantee the free play of individual interests, needed to concern itself with the health of the social organism as a whole. In the United States, Woodrow Wilson, criticizing the American constitution, likened society to 'a living thing . . . shaped to its functions by the sheer pressure of life . . . No living thing can have its organs offset against each other as checks and live.'[15] According to Hegelian philosophy, progress consisted in the growth of social consciousness or social reason. The conflict between the individual and the state – which lay at the heart of classic liberalism – was dissolved by the formula that the individual can realize his potential only as part of society; that individual wishes are rational only to the extent that they are directed towards the good of the whole. The importance of this formula was not just that it detached freedom from governmental non-interference, and reason from material self-interest, but that it also located the principle of rational action in the state – seen as the embodiment of the general will – rather than in the interplay, or even aggregation, of the dispersed preferences of its inhabitants. 'It is as a State . . . that a social organism becomes most distinctly conscious of its existence as an organism'.[16] It was a short step from this to the notion that the general will is best embodied in a government of resourceful minorities and disinterested experts, likened by J. A. Hobson to the nerve centre of an organism. Societies should be directed by centralized will, knowledge and intelligence to their teleological ends. These ideas were mostly developed by liberal professors who had no inkling of their murderous potential.

At the heart of 'scientific' collectivism was the assumption that there existed a standard of social welfare which was separable from the sum of private interests and could not therefore result from the free play of individual initiative or voluntary association. Collectivists looked to the social sciences and to supposedly scientific morals to tell them what this standard was. Yet at this very time the Italian economist Vilfredo Pareto was demonstrating with great clarity the impossibility of moving from a concept of individual (or subjective) utility to one of 'utility of the species'. What, Pareto asked, is a 'healthy' society? Is it one in which the greatest number enjoy material well-being? Or is it one which covers itself with military glory? 'There is no criterion', Pareto wrote, 'which I could apply to determine which of us is right and which wrong.' Collectivists got round the problem by assuming a community with standard, ascertainable needs – material, ethical, psychological. This was the belief which was to drive the central planners right through the era of Communism.

The mind-set of collectivism already existed before 1914, but the actual apparatus of collectivism was in its infancy. Tariffs were widely used to influence the structure of production and supposedly steady employment, but they were set at a low level, and quotas, discrimination and competitive devaluations were unknown. There were a few state monopolies – partly ancient, partly modern – but otherwise little encroachment on private property. Redistributionary taxation had barely started, and state spending on compulsory social-insurance schemes was a tiny fraction of national income. Socialists were unable to give a clear idea of how a publicly owned economy would work; the concept of national planning did not exist. In spite of the alarmist mood, the transition from rural to urban life, from family firms to large corporations, from oligarchic to democratic politics, seems to have proceeded with amazing smoothness. Even the tensions created by the spread of imperialism proved negotiable. In one of those swings which are a constant feature of the collectivist age, there was a liberal revival after the recovery from depression in 1896. The economist John Maynard Keynes, looking back in 1919 at the years immediately before the outbreak of war, dismissed the domestic and international horrors now emphasized by historians as the 'amusements of the daily newspaper', which 'appeared to exercise no influence at all on the ordinary course of social and economic life'. His pre-war Europe was an 'economic eldorado', peopled by citizens reasonably content with their lot, in which there existed 'an almost absolute security of property and persons'.[17] All this was ended in 1914.

CHAPTER FOUR

THE ERA OF WARS

The First World War was the great watershed. Before the war there were collectivist dreams; after it, collectivist projects, which turned into collectivist nightmares. The war seemingly disclosed a world of reality which corresponded to the world of the collectivist imagination; it showed that collectivist organization worked, and it created revolutionary situations which enabled collectivists to seize power.

War has thus been a powerful agent of collectivism. But it must never be forgotten that wars are as much a product as a cause of collectivist thinking. There was nothing in the state of international relations before 1914 to cause the great powers of Europe to inflict four years of mass murder on their conscripted subjects. No one was threatening anyone. The war was born in the imagination of rulers; once started, it enlisted the forces of nationalism on its behalf, and could not be stopped.

In his *Imperialism and Social Classes* (1919), Joseph Schumpeter linked the warlike imagination to a particular kind of social structure – one dominated by a military aristocracy. The carrier of imperialist ventures was the 'machine of warriors, created by wars that required it, which now creates the wars it requires'. This fitted the case of Germany particularly well. As German historians tell it, foreign policy was used to achieve social integration by a semi-feudal dynastic state which could not democratize itself. The high-tariff policy which Germany started in 1879 to protect its agriculture and heavy industry, and the naval race with Britain begun in 1902, cut across normal trade and capital flows, creating a circle of hostility to the German Empire which the German militarists came to believe had to be dispersed by force before it became too powerful.

The lesson Schumpeter drew is that the more 'bourgeois' states become in their domestic organization, the less they will be inclined to view their relations with others in doom-laden ways. This should be reassuring to those who fear today that the re-unification of Germany will recreate the 'German problem' as it has existed historically.

The First World War disclosed for the first time the techniques by which the economic and political life of a society might be effectively directed by the state. Lenin saw the German war economy as a blueprint for socialist organization. What it did was to provide an alternative to the price mechanism for allocating resources. Direct production orders were placed by the military, and labour and raw materials were allocated by ministries of munitions to secure their delivery. Here was the nucleus of the planning system. Another innovation was the inflation tax. Governments discovered that they could transfer resources to themselves without raising taxes by printing money. With the extra money the government could buy more goods; because of the rise in prices, the public could buy less. The process could continue a long time if the printing presses kept ahead of wages. Only at extremely high levels of inflation does the tax become ineffective: no one is willing to accept the government's paper, so it can't buy anything with it. In Central and Eastern Europe wartime inflation gave way, in the first years of peace, to hyperinflation and currency collapses. The whole *funeste* process would start up again in the 1970s, when governments which could not honestly pay for the entitlements they had created resorted once more to this most seductive of taxes.[1]

The war promoted social cohesion and a philosophy of 'fair shares', even while abrogating civil, political and industrial liberties. This made it an attractive precedent for those who saw democracy, or trade unions, or private owners, or a free press, as an impediment to their designs. To socialists the war proved that capitalism was warlike, and had to be suppressed; to the Right it showed that national solidarity could overcome class conflict.

Thus, instead of war organization being thought an exception to the normal way in which societies earned their living, it impressed many people as a model. Reviewing the experience of British wartime planning in 1932, Arthur Salter wrote, 'The results . . . were amazing. At a moderate estimate, between a half and two-thirds of the productive capacity of the country was withdrawn into combatant or other war service. And yet, throughout the war, Great Britain sustained the whole of her military effort and maintained the civilian population at a standard of life which was never intolerably low, and for some periods and for some classes as comfortable as in times of peace.'[2] The question that got asked after the war was, If the state can organize society for war, why not for peace? The answer is obvious: in war there is a clear priority and a general will to achieve it. In peace there is no priority, only preferences.

The First World War also created the revolutionary situations which enabled the Bolsheviks to seize power in Russia in 1917 and Mussolini to seize power in Italy in 1922. These usurpations split the collectivist movement much more sharply than before into its reformist (liberal, democratic) and its revolutionary (totalitarian) wings. Until 1914 there was no explicit repudiation of political democracy. Even the Bolsheviks thought of revolution as merely giving a final push to an industrial society ripe for Communism. However, Lenin seized power in a country of peasants, and declared the 'dictatorship of the proletariat'. At best this could only mean the rule of the small minority of industrial workers over the vast majority of peasants; in practice, the revolution was intended to install the dictatorship of the Communist Party, as Lenin made clear in his pamphlet *The State and Revolution* (1917). Emboldened and influenced by Lenin (all dictators are keen students of each other's 'form'), Mussolini was the first leader in history to make totalitarianism his explicit aim. His essay on the 'doctrine of Fascism', written in 1929 by the philosopher Giovanni Gentile, combines an organicist-idealist theory of the state – 'outside of it no human or spiritual values can exist, much less have value' – with the two most important conclusions of late-nineteenth-century 'realist' political thought: the law of struggle and the law of minority rule. The first denied the possibility of permanent peace; the second proclaimed that democracy was bound to be a sham. Liberalism was rejected not just because of its supposedly false philosophical premises (the individual comes first) but because it weakened the state against predatory interests, domestic or foreign. Parliamentary democracy (the counting of heads) was replaced by the notion of a 'general will' embodied and articulated by the leader. 'All the experiments of our day are anti-liberal,' said Mussolini. In place of the exhausted doctrines of democracy, liberalism and socialism, he proposed a 'party governing a nation "totalitarianly" '. Fascism was the instrument by which Italy would realize its destiny: 'imperialism implies discipline, the coordination of efforts, a deep sense of duty and a spirit of self-sacrifice. This explains many aspects of the practical activity of the regime, and the direction taken by many of the forces of the State, as also the severity which has to be exercised towards those who . . . oppose [it].'[3]

One of the great historical blindspots has been the assumption that Fascism perished in 1945. In fact it was the progenitor not only of Francoism in Spain but of Perónism in Argentina, and of much of the political and economic theory of the 'developmental state'. In many respects Fascism proved a better model for developing countries than Communism, since it enabled state control to be established without nationalizing the whole economy.

Fascism also provided a rhetoric of nationalism particularly suitable for anti-colonial use. It was Mussolini who invented the concept of the 'proletarian' nation being exploited by Anglo-American imperialism. This formula neatly bypassed the domestic class struggle. Marxists said that there would have to be two revolutions against colonialism: the national bourgeois revolution and the class revolution. Fascism stopped at the first. The concept of the national revolution led on naturally to the doctrine of self-sufficiency – the key to both welfare and power in a world in which power relations were assumed to be always determining. Capitalist market economy was seen as either Utopian or Machiavellian – an unrealistic or fraudulent prospectus. The First World War had stripped away both the liberal illusion and the liberal mask.

The regressive potential of these totalitarian projects was not immediately realized. Indeed the general restoration of peace between 1918 and 1921 saw a retreat from the militarized economy, even in Communist Russia. Between 1917 and 1920 when the Bolshevik armies were fighting a civil war for the control of Russia, a system of 'war Communism' was instituted. This was basically a crude method of requisitioning factory stocks and peasant surpluses to provision the Red armies – something which armies have done throughout history. State ownership developed chaotically as workers seized the factories and peasants seized the land, expelling or murdering their old owners; money exchange broke down because of hyperinflation. The Bolshevik solution to these problems was dictatorial control over the factories, forced requisitions from the peasants, and distribution of basic goods to town-dwellers either free or at fixed prices. Once the civil war was won, this system broke down, because the peasants (80 per cent of the population) not the Communists controlled the land, and, despite state-sponsored terror, refused to deliver food to the towns on the Communist Party's terms. So, in March 1921, the Tenth Party Congress, reversing track, adopted the 'New Economic Policy', which allowed market relations based on private ownership between town and country outside heavy industry. The NEP was started to legitimize what could not be controlled. It lasted until 1929.

Gorbachev would look back to the NEP as an inspiration for his own reforms. What it did was to sanction a revival of rural capitalism. Peasants were confirmed in their land as leaseholders; requisitions of surpluses were replaced by 'the tax in kind'; any post-tax surpluses could be sold on the open market. 'The *kulak* [rich peasant] produced for the market and became a small capitalist; this was the essence of NEP.'[4] Small private firms were encouraged to produce for the rural market, and

even larger ones were leased out, sometimes back to their previous owners. State industry was organized into trusts, with the
factories run by 'specialists' of the old regime. Essential industries like coal, metal goods, electricity and armaments remained
under direct central control and had to deliver their produce
to the state; otherwise, trusts were free to sell off their products
at market prices which covered costs, including a return to capital (profit) which had to be paid to the state. Electricity was
planned, much as the tsars had planned the railways, Lenin
coining the phrase 'Communism is soviet power, plus electri-
fication.' The rouble was stabilized in 1924, a stock exchange
was established in Moscow, the money economy revived, and a
new class of merchants – Nepmen – came to dominate the retail
market. In the heyday of the NEP, in the mid-1920s, the share
of the private sector in the national income was over 50 per
cent.

The start of the New Economic Policy suggested the possibility of reintegrating Soviet Russia into the world economic
community. At Genoa in April 1922, Keynes advocated a £50
million British credit to the Soviets 'to promote agricultural
production, whether tools and machinery or for the improvement of communications, with the purpose of ameliorating the
Russian famine in the first instance and encouraging export
thereafter'.[5] He made contact with Yevgenii Preobrazhensky,
later the architect of Stalinist economics. Preobrazhensky, like
Trotsky, wanted to secure an investment fund from the export
of food and raw materials to pay for imports of capital equipment for industrialization. So there was clearly a possibility of
a deal between Soviet Russia and the West. No deal was made,
because the question of tsarist debts was a decisive obstacle to
the issue of the credits Keynes wanted. Nineteen twenty-two
was a hinge year. Could long-term Western credits to enable
the resumption of Soviet grain exports have prevented the final
radicalization of the Bolshevik Revolution under Stalin? We
will never know.

The most interesting contemporary comment on the NEP

is Keynes's *Short View of Soviet Russia*, written after a visit there in 1925. Keynes describes 'a certain equilibrium' in the Russian economy between on the one hand an urban proletariat of 20 million living at a higher standard than its output justifies and on the other 120 million peasants exploited by the towns, but accepting this because of their *de facto* ownership of the land. Exploitation was accomplished by the state's procurement policy. Their import and export monopoly and virtual control of industrial output enabled 'the authorities to maintain relative prices at levels highly disadvantageous to the peasant. They buy his wheat from him much below the world price, and they sell him textile and other manufactured goods appreciably above the world price, the difference providing a fund out of which can be financed their high overhead costs and the general inefficiency of manufacture and distribution'. Earlier he had noted that import controls enabled the Soviets to maintain an overvalued exchange rate despite inflationary domestic finance.[6]

Keynes identified five interrelated components of the Soviet regime's management of its economy under the NEP: state monopoly of the import and export trade; the inflation tax; an overvalued currency; the distortion of relative prices which turned the internal terms of trade against agricultural producers; and state subsidies for government-owned industries. As John Toye has pointed out, these five features were to form the core of the economic policies of most developing countries in the 1970s.[7] Keynes concluded that Soviet Russia's economy required 'structural adjustment': paying the peasant the market price for his produce would stimulate higher output and stop the excessive migration from the countryside to the towns produced by artificially high urban wages. In other words, Keynes rejected the policy of state-led industrialization. Whether writing about Russia or India, he stuck to the liberal doctrine of comparative advantage: Russia's lay in its low-cost agriculture and light consumer goods, not in capital-intensive industry.

The abandonment of war Communism in the Soviet Union

had its parallel in the attempts of other European countries to 'get back to normalcy' after the traumatic interlude of war. Although statesmen were half-conscious that the war had created a new age, the only way they knew how to run their countries – or indeed world affairs – was according to the precepts of the old age. Rulers tried to reimpose the 'disciplines of the market' – the gold standard and free trade – on societies whose industrial relations had become much stickier as a result of the war. Paradoxically, the only ruler who succeeded was Mussolini. His formula was to lavish praise on the workers while depriving them of their political and trade-union rights – a system of orthodox finance lubricated by flattery and the castor-oil treatment. Socialists in the 1970s predicted that this is what capitalism would be driven to again.

In Continental Europe, particularly Weimar Germany, the attempt to adjust the cartellized industry and heavily unionized workforce promoted by the war to the 'Anglo-Saxon' disciplines of the market led to an explicit corporatist philosophy involving 'the displacement of power from elected representatives or a career bureaucracy to the major organised forces . . .' These corporatist arrangements 'not only helped re-entrench prewar elites, but also rewarded labour leadership and injured the less organized middle-classes'.[8] The American parallel was the trade-association movement, designed to limit competition and overproduction. In Britain the conflict between the restored free-trade gold-standard system and law-enhanced trade-union power resulted in a low-employment equilibrium. The enfeeblement of British industry was the price of social peace.

This sticky system of corporatist coordination was highly intolerant of the demands of the international gold standard as it operated in the 1920s. The pull of world gold reserves to the United States exerted continual deflationary pressure on Europe, mainly because the USA had high protection, and the Europeans had little to sell it that it wanted. The same deflationary forces were felt in Latin America and Australasia in the downward pressure on commodity prices. When the American loans which refloated the postwar economy dried up in 1928, the unstable equilibrium between currency stabilization, free trade and corporatism broke down.

The years 1929–33 were the second great watershed in the development of collectivism. In the Soviet Union, Stalin liquidated the New Economic Policy and forcibly collectivized the farms; elsewhere, capitalism collapsed into the Great Depression. Political and economic liberty were virtually extinguished in four great powers (Germany, Italy, Japan and the USSR), and collectivism was given a boost the world over. In all countries, foreign trade was heavily controlled, governments intervened to limit domestic competition, national planning became the fashionable doctrine of the day. The Cobdenite world of free trade and *laissez-faire* seemed as dead as the dodo.

The 1930s confront us with a puzzle. Why did two largely disconnected systems – capitalism and Communism – shift towards radical collectivism at the same time? If one is looking for a single proximate explanation for both forced collectivization and the Great Depression, the likeliest candidate is the collapse in the price of grain in 1929 – the interwar equivalent of the OPEC oil-price shock of 1973–4. Between 1929 and 1931 the world price of wheat fell by 40 per cent. Since grain was Russia's main export, this put paid to 'primitive socialist accumulation' from the export sector. At the same time it ruined the American farming community, reducing demand for manufactured goods.

But, just as in the 1970s, the change in a single price would not have had the profound repercussions it did had not the prevailing systems of political economy already been in deep trouble. The fact is that the disequilibria caused by the First World War had never been corrected. In the USSR the New Economic Policy was riddled with ideological and economic contradictions. By the late 1920s the policy of exploiting the peasants was breaking down. Rather than sell grain to the state at fixed prices, the peasants restricted supply to get better prices from the state, sold on the black market, or turned their grain to other uses, like distilling alcohol. In 1928, black-market prices were 40 per cent above official prices. The authorities fixed retail prices of consumer goods in order to reduce wage pressure. This emptied the shops without stopping wage inflation, and left the Nepmen in control of the retail trade. As a result there was no net transfer from agriculture to industry or from wages to profits over the lifetime of the NEP. So there was the familiar crisis which hits all halfway-house economic systems sooner or later: whether to advance to full-blooded control or to allow the market to work.

Over the opposition of Trotsky and Bukharin, the NEP started to be dismantled in 1927. The kulaks and Nepmen were denounced as 'profiteers'; the area of market relations was progressively restricted, the area of planning was enlarged, and increasing coercion was applied in the countryside and in the factories. This bred resistance, requiring more coercion. From 1927 the regime started to take on its Stalinist features, as Stalin himself rose to supremacy. The law was used to round up enemies of the regime. The party and state apparatus were merged in a supreme Politburo. Open debate was ended, and the press was allowed to print only the official party line. Oppositionists were denounced and exiled. Show trials began. All this was justified in the name of concentrating the energy and will of Soviet society on a single aim: industrialization. Once the first five-year plan was approved, in March 1929, the position of the peasants outside the plan became anomalous, since industrialization called for increased food supplies to the cities. First, the war-Communism policy of forced requisitions was reimposed; finally, in January 1930, the incorporation of all the peasant holdings into giant food-production 'factories' and the 'liquidation of the kulaks as a class' were decreed. Between 1930 and 1933 millions of peasants were murdered or died of starvation as agricultural output plummeted – uniquely in the world. These 'successes' of Soviet planning, coupled with mass unemployment in the capitalist world, 'encouraged a growing belief [in the West] that no national economy could any longer be left at the mercy of the iron laws of the market. The Soviet five-year plan . . . seemed to provide a pioneering model.'⁹

It would be quite wrong to say that Stalinism was caused by contradictions in the NEP. Contradictions offered a choice between a market-oriented strategy of agricultural development, such as Keynes advocated in 1925, and a shift to radical collectivism. It was the mind-set of most Bolsheviks which prevented the first strategy being pursued – the crude association of welfare with heavy industry; the need to justify a proletarian revolution by turning peasants into proletarians as quickly as possible; above all, the paranoia of 'encirclement', like Germany's before 1914. Stalin was paranoid, but paranoia is inherent in illegitimate power. The tyrant feels himself surrounded by enemies, because he is. He creates the enemies his tyranny has to guard against. So he is forced to embark on a relentless quest to make himself absolute master at home, and his state impregnable against its enemies abroad. By actions which repelled the West and oppressed their own subjects, the Bolshevik leaders were driven to terror to safeguard their security, which they identified with the security of the state and the revolution.

Against this, an *ex post facto* argument is often used. The insane haste of Soviet industrialization 'enabl[ed] the Soviet Union to withstand and eventually turn back, the massive assault by Nazi Germany in 1941'.¹⁰ This stands the argument on its head. If a state, through methods of terror, denudes itself of allies, it has no alternative but to rely on its own resources for its defence. The European balance of power in the 1930s would have been completely different with a more 'normal' Russian state. Apologists for Stalin have always argued that Stalin's methods were necessary to achieve the security of the Soviet state. Whether the security of the Soviet state was best for the security or welfare of its people is precisely the question being begged.

If the First World War left economic liberalism reeling, the Great Depression of the 1930s was virtually a knockout blow.

The background to the shift to collectivism in the West was the scale of collapse of capitalist industrial output and agricultural prices: 37 per cent in the former, 55 per cent in the latter over the three years 1929–32. The two events, war and depression, are linked together as cause and effect, yet the train of causation and the interaction of different pathologies at each stage are too complicated to be captured by any model. The internal collapse of the United States in 1929–30 was the most dramatic event, as America had replaced Britain as the dominant capitalist power. But it was the failure of the US monetary authorities to offset the fall in prices, particularly of agricultural and raw-material products, which seems to have been decisive in converting a serious recession into a catastrophic depression. As Keynes put it in 1933, 'it was . . . the collapse of expenditure financed out of loans advanced by the United States, for use both at home and abroad, which was the chief agency in starting the slump'.[11]

One gets a little closer to an understanding if one reflects that the war had shattered the economic unity of pre-war Europe, thereby disrupting its means of earning its livelihood. In the *Economic Consequences of the Peace* (1919), Keynes had observed that the territories of the 300 million people of Germany, Austro-Hungary and Russia comprised a single economic zone in which 'the interference of frontiers and tariffs was reduced to a minimum', stable currencies 'facilitated the easy flow of capital and of trade', and 'there was an almost absolute security of property and person'. These factors enabled the development of 'that vast mechanism of transport, coal distribution, and foreign trade which made possible an industrial order of life in the dense urban centres of new population'. Round Germany as a central support 'the rest of the European economic system grouped itself'. In modern language, Germany was the 'locomotive' of the European economy, supplying its neighbours with much of their exports and capital, and taking most of their imports. Even Britain and France with their wider trading networks were heavily interdependent with Germany:

Germany was Britain's second-, and France's third-best customer, and the second largest supplier to both countries.[12]

Keynes foresaw that the territorial fragmentation produced by the war, the Bolshevik Revolution in Russia, and the foolish policy of lopping off bits of Germany without regard to industrial linkages would seriously damage the 'delicate organisation by which these peoples lived'. So it turned out. The weakening of the industrial heart of Europe in turn weakened the limbs – Western Europe's peripheries in Eastern Europe, Latin America and Asia, which had depended on the major European states to take their exports of food and raw materials and to provide them with capital. The disruption of the European-based world economy left a highly artificial situation in which the avoidance of a severe decline in the real incomes of the nations locked by history into this sophisticated trading system became dependent on capital exports from the United States, whose involvement in world trade was small and which excluded from its own shores most of the goods by which its debtors might hope to repay their debts. A world depression became inevitable when the United States cut down on lending and imports at the same time between 1928 and 1930.

The greatest mystery of all is the scale of the economic downturn in the United States, whose industrial output declined by over 40 per cent between 1929 and 1932. One clue is the collapse of world wheat prices in 1929. The United States, as Charles Kindleberger has reminded us, was one of the major producers as well as exporters of agricultural products, so the withdrawal of US financial support for stocks which kept up the wheat price reduced the incomes, while increasing the real value of farm debt, of its own farming communities, as well as of those in Canada, Australasia and Latin America. Kindleberger thinks it an 'open question whether an independent depression in agriculture helped cause the stock-market crash, the decline in industrial output and the banking collapse' in the United States.[13]

It has been argued that an expansionary monetary policy

could have averted the calamity. Certainly the monetary policies of various countries – Britain when it returned to the gold
standard in 1925 at an overvalued exchange rate with the dollar,
the United States and France in 1929–30 – took little account
of the growing rigidity of domestic economies. A competitive
scramble for gold, exacerbated by the war-debts imbroglio
and misaligned exchange rates, replaced the British-managed
gold standard of the pre-1914 era. When the crunch came in
1929–30, Britain could not and the USA would not take steps
to prevent the collapse of the world money supply.[14] But it has
to be said that, in view of the political, economic and monetary
derangement wrought by the war, monetary policy was called
on to perform a much more heroic task than had been required
in the nineteenth century – one for which prevailing ideas and
politics were quite unsuitable.

Whatever the causes, the consequences of the Great Depression were indisputable. In the face of collapsing prices and
output and rising unemployment, all governments started to
intervene to limit competition and to plan trade. Domestically,
their chief (if misguided) object was to maintain prices and profits by concentrating industry and reducing supply. In external
policy, every country in a position to do so tried to break or
control the link between national welfare and international
trade, by means of tariffs, quotas, competitive devaluations, capital and foreign exchange controls, international cartels, and bilateral clearing and payments arrangements. As a result, the
world broke up into a group of economic blocs. These were
mainly piecemeal adjustments to shocks. However, the Depression also produced a fully articulated alternative to the
nineteenth-century liberal economic order: the doctrine of
self-sufficiency. This became the spoken aim of the Fascist
powers, and the unspoken one of many of the others. It survived
beyond the Second World War in the industrializing strategies
of developing countries.

The Great Depression gave Hitler the chance to win power
in Germany in January 1933. His wordy manifesto, *Mein
Kampf*, published in 1924, shows him heir to all the Social Dar-

winist, Machiavellian and pan-German ideas which had flourished in Central Europe before the First World War. The nub of his argument was that the 'welfare of our people' could be secured only by foreign policy, and that an internal revolution was needed for the sake of a strong foreign policy. Germany had lost the war because the moribund imperial regime and disintegrative liberal values had prevented the effective organization of the German people to win the *Lebensraum*, or 'living-space', required to secure its existence. To mobilize and organize the nation to realize its destiny was the historic task of the National Socialist Party and its leader. For Hitler, national welfare depended on ensuring a 'healthy and natural proportion between the number and growth of the population . . . and the extent and the resources of the territory they inhabit'. So the object of German foreign policy must be to secure an expanded 'living-space' at the expense of Russia and its border states, which, according to Hitler, were ripe for dissolution. The economic argument that Germany could not feed its expanding population without an expanded *Lebensraum* was claptrap, although it was also used by Mussolini to justify the Italian attack on Abyssinia in 1935, and by the Japanese to rationalize their seizure of Manchuria in 1932. (All three regimes embarked on a population policy designed to produce more soldiers to acquire the land to produce more soldiers.)

More poignant was the evocation by all three Fascist regimes of the powerful image of the 'closing frontier'. Alexander Hamilton and Friedrich List, the nineteenth-century theorists of economic nationalism, writing in agricultural communities, had argued that the healthy development of a nation required the encouragement of the manufacturing industry. Hitler, following Adolph Wagner, saw the task rather as deindustrializing Germany by settling more of its population on the soil. Unfortunately, more heavy industry was needed to produce the armaments necessary to win new soil. This irony was given a macabre twist when the Allies in 1944 accepted (temporarily as it turned out) Hitler's programme of repastoralizing German society as a guarantee against future German aggression, though in a much smaller 'living-space' than Hitler had set out to win.

These ideas preceded the Great Depression. They are buried in the subconscious of late-nineteenth-century Europe. What the Great Depression did was to confirm to people like Hitler and Mussolini that the world as they had always imagined it to be was the world that was actually taking shape. The Hawley-Smoot tariff put up by the United States in 1930, which set customs duties for many manufactured goods at over 60 per cent; the British abandonment of free trade in 1932 for protection, imperial preference and a sterling-area payments union; the Dutch closure of the East Indies to Japanese textile exports in 1933 all showed that the international division of labour, and the pacifist illusions founded on it, were dead. The hour for medium-sized great powers to seize their 'place in the sun' had struck.

Latin versions of self-sufficiency, inspired by Mussolini and the political philosophy of 'caudillismo', spread to Spain, Argentina and Brazil. Spain's civil-war victor Franco spoke for them all when he declared in 1939, 'Our victory constitutes the triumph of economic principles opposed to old liberal theories whose myths support a colonial domination over sovereign states.' Spain embarked on a programme of import substitution and forced industrialization regardless of cost. 'A vast armoury of bureaucratic instruments, created in the war economy of 1936–9, was now deployed in the attempt to create a self-sustained economy.'[15]

It is often forgotten now that the social experiment which seemed at the time closest in spirit to Hitler's recovery programme was Roosevelt's New Deal in the United States. John Garraty has written a fascinating study of the political techniques, rhetoric and anti-depression policies of the two leaders, showing how similar they were. Both undertook big works-creation programmes which involved millions of people building roads, schools, bridges, etc. (The American term 'boondoggle', meaning a useless project, had its parallel in what the Germans called *Pyramidenbau*; Keynes, too, commended the pharaonic solution to unemployment.) Both policies involved military spending: the American Public Works Administration spent close to a billion dollars on armaments. Both regimes instituted work camps, designed to keep young men out of the labour market and organized on semi-military lines. Both the Nazis and the New Dealers cosseted labour. The Nazis destroyed independent unions, but much of their industrial and social policy was pro-worker. Roosevelt was unenthusiastic about Senator Wagner's Labour Relations Act of 1935, which guaranteed the right to unionize; the administration-inspired Social Security Act of 1935 and Fair Labour Standards Act of 1940 were designed to benefit workers, not union members. Both Roosevelt and Hitler 'tended to idealize rural life' and started pro-agricultural policies, though their efforts at promoting land resettlement were equally disappointing. Both used propaganda, including the cinema, to sell their policies. 'Like the Nazi swastika . . . the Blue Eagle [symbol of the National Recovery Administration] was plastered everywhere.' General 'Ironpants' Johnson, head of the NRA and designer of the Blue Eagle, proclaimed that 'Those who are not with us are against us . . . The way to show that you are part of this great army of the New Deal is to insist on this symbol of solidarity.' That the war against unemployment was a *war*, demanding the same effort at mobilizing society under a powerful leader, was a common theme of both systems.[16] There were two crucial differences: for Hitler, unlike for Roosevelt, the rhetorical war against unemployment was a preparation for the real war to secure Germany's 'living-space', and his power was untramelled by constitutional checks. That is why Nazi collectivism went on expanding, while Roosevelt's started to go into reverse. This was particularly true in two areas: corporatism and economic nationalism.

According to Garraty, 'production controls to prevent gluts, limitation of entry of new companies to lessen competition, and price and wage manipulation were characteristics of industrial policy in both countries'.[17] The Nazis created thirteen compulsory cartels governing all branches of industry under the control of the minister of economics. The early New Deal's National Recovery Administration (1933) expressed the same corporatist, or 'associational', intent. It set up self-policing government–industry planning agreements for the main industrial sectors, designed to limit production and fix prices, provide minimum wages and maximum hours of work, and guarantee workers' rights to form unions and bargain collectively. Both Rex Tugwell and Adolf Berle, two members of Roosevelt's first Brain Trust, wanted to go much further. Tugwell envisaged a planning board for each industry. On top of this would come a central planning board staffed by disinterested experts, allocating capital and controlling prices. In practice the NRA favoured big business interests, and, after the Supreme Court declared the NRA unconstitutional in 1935, the older anti-trust doctrine made a comeback. The New Deal's corporatist projects harked back to pre-1914 critiques of big business which had little relevance to the general collapse of spending power brought about by the Great Depression. After the recession of 1937, the emphasis gradually shifted to stimulation of aggregate spending as Keynesian ideas took hold, but not before a young Harvard economist, John Kenneth Galbraith, had co-authored a book calling for 'the mandatory participation of poorly performing corporations in a system of mild indicative planning coordinated by a congressionally appointed committee'.[18] In Germany, by contrast, central planning went forward with the first four-year-plan, in 1936. This was because the Germans were preparing for war.

Both Hitler's and Roosevelt's early policies were inspired by economic nationalism. Hjalmar Schacht, Hitler's economic wizard, praised Roosevelt for 'torpedoing' the World Economic Conference of 1933, called to re-establish fixed exchange rates following the collapse of the gold standard in 1931. In Schacht's system of managed trade, Germany signed bilateral agreements with Eastern European countries to buy grain and energy at fixed prices in return for supplying manufactures. In 1936 Schacht expanded the bartering system. Roosevelt toyed with the same ideas, but finally came down in favour of reciprocal tariff concessions within a restored fixed-exchange-rate framework. In essence, a combination of the United States constitution and the perceived distinction between a crisis and normal times pulled the United States back from the brink of collectivism; there were no such barriers in Hitler's Germany.

Self-sufficiency was the distinctive Fascist contribution to the economic ideology of collectivism, though it was equally practised by the USSR. It went beyond the economic nationalism of List. The two Greek words 'autarky' and 'autarchy' were used interchangeably to describe the doctrine, but '*autarkeia*' literally means 'self-sufficiency', whereas '*autarchia*' means 'autocracy', 'despotism' or else 'self-government'. In the 1930s, the drive to self-sufficiency, or autarky, was founded on the desire to achieve *autarchia*, or power to control one's own destiny, generally by states which were despotic in their internal politics and felt victimized internationally.

The ostensible starting-point for autarkic states of mind was the belief that reliance on international exchange subjected domestic economies to fluctuations outside their control but which in principle might be controlled. Immunity against the trade cycle was seen as one big advantage. The other was immunity against the instruments of 'colonial domination'. Germany had been the victim of successful blockade in the First World War; Italy was subject to 'sanctions' in 1935. 'Dependence on the goodwill of foreigners', Goering said, 'is for a self-conscious people that has the desire to live, simply intolerable.' The circular nature of the reasoning is apparent: both countries, acting on the assumption that the world was inherently insecure, provoked reactions from others which then justified them in acting in that way.

Fear of starvation in war, as well as belief in the mystical qualities of soil, spurred the Fascist states to efforts at agricultural self-sufficiency: Mussolini's 'battle for wheat' was one example. They also lavished research on the invention of substitutes. The Italians encouraged development of a new textile fibre made from skimmed milk. State industries needed to be set up to do this. Such efforts have a long history: the development of beet sugar in Europe as a substitute for cane sugar goes back to the Napoleonic wars. The USSR manufactured synthetic rubber. With security rather than higher living standards the aim, price was no object.

The problem for apostles of self-sufficiency was that except for the largest countries, like the United States and the Soviet Union, domestic self-sufficiency was impossible. The success of German and Italian autarkic policies depended on trade links with countries they did not control, so small states had to be made to adapt their economies to the needs of larger and more powerful neighbours. German trade policy was designed to create such close links with the countries of South-East Europe that escape into wider intercourse was impossible. Governments of these countries were expected to supply Germany in bulk with what it needed at fixed prices. But even these countries could not supply all German needs. As one contemporary wrote, 'the search for areas from which essential supplies can be drawn without any necessity for dependence upon the goodwill of foreigners means continuous expansion of the range of control'. It would also preclude relations with third countries trying to do the same thing. 'Any attempt to carve the earth's surface into suitable large-scale autarkic blocs must, it is fairly clear, mean serious conflict.'[19]

The demand that British protectionism be developed into a conscious policy of imperial self-sufficiency was put forward most strongly by Right-wingers like Leo Amery in his book *The Forward View* (1934). 'Economic nationalism is inevitably destined to be the dominating conception of the coming generation, and it is only those who are prepared to accept that fact, and to shape it to their own ends, who can hope to control the future.' The conception of the whole world 'conceived of as a single unit' for promiscuous economic intercourse ignored the clash of economic interests and the 'enduring reality' of nations as 'historic entities, organic structures, ends in themselves'. What was geopolitically right – 'agriculture', Amery wrote, 'had to be protected as the best breeding ground for sturdy recruits' – had now been proved to be economically rational. Scientific progress had weakened the arguments for the international division of labour; problems of 'national employment' were prior to 'international profits'. But the technical requirements of modern production mean that economic nationalism can be constructed only on a bloc basis, 'by widening [national] boundaries, by bringing together nations in groups large enough to satisfy the technical requirements of modern production, and yet also sufficiently held together by some common ideal, some permanent co-operative purpose, to enlist the forces of economic nationalism on their behalf'. Amery cited the United States (or the American hemisphere) as an example of one such bloc, the Soviet Union as another. A future 'European Commonwealth' would be a third, and the British Empire a fourth.[20] Amery's ideas were influential, but not decisive; in any event, they pointed to managed trade rather than absolute self-sufficiency. There are many echoes of Amery today.

The Left's reply to imperial self-sufficiency was planning. G. D. H. Cole, a leading British Labour Party intellectual, agreed with the autarkists that 'the old free trade era has definitely gone, and can never be restored'. The only question was whether the planning of trade was done on a capitalist (imperialist) or a socialist basis. International planning should take the form of encouraging 'large-scale bargains for the exchange of goods wherever these are of such a nature as to be of benefit to both parties to the transaction' – roughly what Schacht was doing. International planning, Cole pointed out, depended on national planning. In order to place orders for definite quantities of goods, a country must know what it will produce at home. It must therefore have a national plan of production under which 'the available resources of materials, machinery, and man-power are definitely assigned to different branches of production, as they are [in] the Soviet Union.' National planning in turn presupposed the administrative allocation of capital. 'A country cannot have a national economic plan unless it is in a position to guide the investment of capital into those industries in which the plan requires the provision of additional capital resources, and to prevent the dissipation of investments in services not scheduled for development under the plan.'[21]

Cole's argument is a good example of the logic of collectivist creep described by the economist Lionel Robbins. Tariffs tend to be replaced by quotas as a 'flood of cheap imports wash across the tariff barriers'; exports become subject to centralized marketing arrangements in the hope of favourably affecting the value of sales; domestic industries are nationalized to assist national planning; control of production in one sector of the economy makes it necessary to control production in all connected branches; the creation of new industry must also be controlled, and this requires the long-term control of investment which requires the nationalization of domestic savings. If one state provides a significantly higher level of benefits to its inhabitants, foreigners will flock in; if its standard of living is relatively low, its own citizens will leave. So immigration and emigration must be controlled too.[22]

The American columnist Walter Lippmann offered a dispassionate summing-up of the collectivist mind-set of the 1930s. Economic nationalists, he wrote, were deeply worried by the fear of disturbances to the domestic order originating in uncontrollable external forces, economic or political. The more entangled countries are in the international system, the less they feel in control of their fate. Economic fear leads to mistrust of international finance: creditors feel that national savings should be invested at home; debtors that foreign capital endangers their independence and humiliates them. Being enmeshed in an international economy prevents countries from experimenting with a more just or more stable social order. 'Thus there is a whole spectrum of fears from military blue to revolutionary red which makes men interested in extricating the national economy from the intrusive and binding forces of interdependence.' Fears are matched by hopes. Those disposed to self-sufficiency believe 'in the beneficent possibilities of a directed and planned social order'. The most perfectly planned society is an army, and planned societies 'whether fascist, communist, or state capitalist all tend to approximate the pattern of military organization: a general staff to do the planning, a hierarch to command, a rank and file under strict discipline'. It is easy to idealize such an order: the civilian is transformed into a civic soldier and endowed with nobler qualities of the military life; he would work not for profit but for the service of the state; he would not indulge the vagaries of the individual mind but think high common thoughts; he would be secure in his status, and 'the whole of which he was a part would be secure because it was disciplined and could therefore be directed without the confusion of debate, of divided opinion, of private ambition, and of private greed'.

Thus, in the logical evolution of the self-sufficient ideal, 'men distrust not only extra-national influences but the intra-national anarchy of individualism. On the other hand they have enormous faith in the capacity of some people to govern others ... to plan the activities of a whole society and then to direct those activities'. A completely planned economy, Lippmann argued, calls for an authoritarian state – for 'the planner must know what men will produce and what they will consume: the only way to make sure of knowing this is to regiment men as producers and ration them as consumers'.

The liberal case against self-sufficiency rested on the advantages of the international division of labour and, more profoundly, on the limits of the human capacity to govern. Prices, liberals argued, are better regulators of human energy than any centralized planning authority could be. However, the success of the liberal system depends upon the flexibility and speed of adjustment to shocks, and this runs up against the fact that most people prefer to live where they have always lived and to do the kind of work they have always done. 'The perfectly free economy requires perfectly mobile human beings.' All interferences with markets are rooted in the conservatism of the human race.

Comparing the two, Lippmann concluded that 'the regimentation by central authority must be weighed in the scales against the anonymous compulsion of markets'. So one must look on the requirements for security and progress as the two poles between which statesmanship has to navigate.[23]

One theme of this chapter has been that the collectivist belief system existed independently of the facts of modern life. The breakdown of the world economy in the 1930s was an inescapable fact, which produced a universal impoverishment. A temporary retrogression of economic and in many cases of political life was an inevitable consequence. The contribution of the doctrine of self-sufficiency was to interpret this retrogression as progress, and to seek to make it the governing principle of a new world order. Defensive arrangements against collapsing output, prices and trade were not viewed as regrettable necessities, but were positively welcomed as harbingers of the scientific control of social life. By 1939, liberal democracy and economic liberalism were endangered species.

Thus, when the European war which broke out in 1939 became general with the German attack on Russia in June 1941, and the Japanese attack on Pearl Harbor in December 1941, the democratic Left, which expected to inherit the fruits of victory, saw the future very much in terms of the generalization of the Soviet system, minus its Stalinist features.

The British Labour Party's vision of postwar life, *The Old World and the New Society* (1941), summed up the experience of the previous half-century as refracted through the lenses of the 'democratic Left'. 'There must be no return', it said, 'to the unplanned competitive world of the inter-war years, in which a privileged few were maintained at the expense of the common good.' In place of competition there would be 'planned production for community use'. Once again, war was lauded as a model for peace in its planning of national life, control of credit, and direction of major national industries and investment. Wartime controls, perpetuated into peace, would be used to counter the 'blind forces of the market'. The 'power of knowledge' would be harnessed to communal effort. A system in which 'the essential instruments of production are privately owned' meant an 'inability to use the full resources of the nation for the benefit of the nation'. 'The nation must own and operate the essential instruments of production.' This will give the community 'the essential instruments of successful planning'. Together with this there would be 'a social service state' based on free medicine, the socialization of insurance, and the provision of public amenities. There would be planned foreign trade and distribution. 'A State which assumes the title to the lives of its citizens owes them the obligation to offer them security while they live.'

CHAPTER FIVE

THE CONVERGENCE OF PATHOLOGIES

That the world after 1945 did not turn out to be the world imagined, or wanted, by the collectivists was due to a number of factors. First, the defeat of the Axis powers had removed the main collectivist challenger, Fascism, from Central and Western Europe. More important even than the military defeat of Fascism was the moral catastrophe it suffered when the full extent of the Nazi genocide of the Jews became known. This horrendous crime inoculated Western Europe against racism, knocked the stuffing out of colonialism, and permanently weakened belief in the European nation-state system. By contrast the Soviet Union and 'Uncle Joe' received much credit for their decisive part in the defeat of Hitlerism. The crimes of Communism, while just as horrendous as those of Fascism, were less vivid to the imagination of the democracies. To this day, the Western public has virtually no visual images of Stalinism, except those produced by Soviet propaganda films. Nevertheless, the revelation at Auschwitz and elsewhere of what totalitarianism can do permanently weakened the appeal to the West of Communism as a political system.

The second factor was the role of the United States in relaunching a liberal form of capitalism. As we have seen, this was bound up with the start of the Cold War. But even before this started the United States brought to postwar problems a free-trade perspective based on the lessons of the 1930s. Once the Cold War began, the United States deliberately promoted the liberalization of the Western European and Japanese economies. Marshall Aid, which ran from 1948 to 1951, disbursed a relatively small amount of money to Europe, $13 billion in all, and not more than 2.5 per cent of the combined national incomes of the recipient countries over the period. It accomplished three things. First, it allowed European countries to avoid deflations or further trade controls in the years of extreme dollar scarcity which followed the Second World War. Secondly, it reoriented them away from socialism and national planning towards capitalism and intra-European trade. A. J. P. Taylor's boast in 1947 that 'nobody in Europe believes in the American way of life – that is, in private enterprise' was obsolete by 1951. Marshall Aid worked to restart West Germany's trade links with its European neighbours. This was the crucial context for Ludwig Erhard's currency stabilization and bonfire of controls which launched West Germany's economic miracle in 1949. Finally, the institutions for channelling Marshall Aid funds, such as the Organization for European Economic Co-operation (OEEC) and the European Payments Union (EPU), led towards the European Economic Community. In Japan, the US occupation accomplished what Marshall Aid did in Europe. In 1947 and 1948 the United States paid for 77 per cent and 68 per cent of Japanese imports. Without this it would have been impossible for 'Japan to finance sufficient imports to avoid starvation among her urban population or to restart many of her industries'.[1] The Socialists who had formed part of a coalition government in 1947 were permanently weakened. In 1950 the Japanese economic miracle started with the heavy procurements of the US Army for the Korean War. Some who argue for a new Marshall Aid for the post-Communist countries forget two things. First, it was the American *military* victory over Germany and Japan which, in conjunction with the start of the Cold War, gave it the incentive and ability to reshape their economic life. Secondly, most of the legal institutions and infrastructure of the capitalist economy had survived their relatively short exposure to Fascism.

The third factor in the anti-collectivist revival was a remarkable wave of liberal intellectual invention directed against the main theses of radical collectivism. Broadly speaking, the intellectual and administrative currents running from the end of the nineteenth century through to the Second World War were all pro-collectivist. The classical liberals, who added nothing significant to their nineteenth-century inheritance, were a beleaguered minority. Liberalism started its fight back in the 1930s. Its capacity for renewal in that moment of seemingly terminal decadence, when all the spiritual and material forces seemed to be on the other side, is astounding testimony to the power of free thought to secure the conditions for its own survival. What emerged was a liberal philosophy whose foundations had been immeasurably strengthened by its engagement with the enemy. It was also one which made far fewer concessions to collectivism than had the 'new liberalism' of the late nineteenth century. A number of pre-eminent thinkers stand out.

The most important is John Maynard Keynes. Keynes explicitly set out to refute the doctrine that only collectivism is capable of guaranteeing full employment. His crucial role in restoring economic liberalism has been obscured for many by the association of Keynesian policies in the 1960s and 1970s with the massive expansion of state activity. This had nothing to do with Keynes, who died in 1946. Despite occasional use of collectivist language, Keynes was never a collectivist in the sense in which I have used the term – someone who wanted to replace private choice by government choice. Keynes wanted to insert governments into the 'gaps' of a free economy – to do things individuals wanted done, but which, in their private transactions, they could not achieve. This is strongly related to the public-goods theory of the state mentioned in chapter 2. As for the rest, Keynes lauded, in almost Hayekian vein, individualistic capitalism as embodying 'the most secure and successful choices of former generations' and being 'the most powerful instrument to better the future'.[2] The question of how this liberal thinker came to be appropriated by the collectivists is something which we will need to address.

The chief 'gap' which Keynes detected in *laissez-faire* was its failure to guarantee continuous employment for all who wanted it. This 'gap' was the result of a mistake in classical economic theory. Traditional theory, which explained how the system of relative prices allocated resources to their preferred uses, was simultaneously a theory of full employment, since, with perfect competition, there was bound to be, at any point in time, a set of prices at which every job-seeker could find work. Keynes did not doubt that such a set of 'equilibrium' prices existed; he denied they could be achieved, or even known, if the economy is violently unstable. Money plays a central role in his theory of economic disturbances. Keynes argued that, in a world of inescapable uncertainty, holding savings in liquid form may be a rational alternative to investing them. If savers, feeling gloomy about the future, decide to invest less of their incomes than they are in the habit of saving, less money is spent buying goods and services, and the effect is felt in a fall in output and prices. Since no one knows what the market-clearing prices for products and labour now are, employers (in industrial sectors) will tend to keep up prices as best they can and sack workers; in agricultural and primary-product sectors it is prices which collapse while output, for a time, is maintained. Either way, national income will fall until a sufficient degree of impover-ishment establishes a new balance between saving and invest-ment, or aggregate supply and demand. Economies can linger in a situation of 'underemployment' for a long time till some-thing turns up which causes entrepreneurs to regain their optimism.*

One of Keynes's key insights was that sensible behaviour by individuals trying to do the best they can for themselves in uncertain circumstances can produce irrational results for so-ciety as a whole – the so-called 'fallacy of composition'. An increased 'propensity to hoard' may be a rational response by individuals to gloomy expectations of profits, but the economy will collapse, and they will be worse off, if everyone tries to

* Technically Keynes established the possibility of 'underemployment equilib-rium'. This is not the same as persisting 'mass unemployment', though that will be the form it normally takes in industrial economies. It means the persisting 'underuse' of capacity, including human capacity. An economy in which university graduates were compelled to work as roadsweepers would be an underemployed economy in Keynes's sense, even if there was no registered unemployment.

hoard more simultaneously. Another insight is that the level of activity in a capitalist economy depends on psychological expectations about the future – and there is nothing to guarantee that these will be consistent with full employment. So it is the government's task to maintain an environment conducive to optimistic expectations – one which encourages businessmen to do their job of creating wealth and jobs. How it is to do this is essentially a second-order question: it depends on the facts of the case. Nothing was more contrary to Keynes's intention than that governments should run permanent budget deficits. Nor was it Keynes's aim to redistribute income, nationalize the economy, or direct investment or the location of industry. His aim was simply to ensure a level of aggregate demand sufficient to enable market-clearing real wages to be established without price inflation. His theory was deliberately designed to make the microeconomic interventions favoured by the planners, regulators and corporatists irrelevant.*

The first chance to apply these ideas came in the Second World War. War is an excuse for every collectivist to get into business; but the emphasis of Keynes's pamphlet *How to Pay for the War* (1940) is markedly libertarian. He rejected physical planning of production and the rationing of distribution, proposing instead that the 'inflationary gap' – the excess of civilian incomes over what was available for private purchase at current prices after government war orders were met – should be closed by a mixture of progressive taxes and deferred pay, a proposal endorsed by Hayek. Private production would be left free to respond to how individuals chose to spend their post-tax incomes; after the war, the release of deferred pay would counteract the anticipated postwar slump 'by allowing individuals to choose themselves what they want [rather than] having to devise large-scale government plans of expenditure which may not correspond so closely to personal need'. The social philosophy underlying this plan was clearly stated:

---

* With one exception: Keynes thought that, under modern conditions, controls over capital movements were required to maintain a fixed-exchange-rate system.

I am not proposing an expedient, undesirable for its own sake, just for the purpose of financing the war. I am seizing an opportunity . . . to introduce a principle of policy which may be thought of as marking the line of division between the totalitarian and the free economy. For if the community's aggregate rate of spending can be regulated, the way in which personal incomes are spent and the means by which demand is satisfied can be safely left free and individual. Just as in the war the regulation of aggregate spending is the only way to avoid the destruction of choice and initiative, whether by the consumer or by producers, through the complex tyranny of all-round rationing, so in peace it is only the application of this principle which will provide the environment in which the choice and initiative of the individual can be safely left free. This is the one kind of compulsion of which the effect is to enlarge liberty.[3]

Keynes also played a key part in establishing the Bretton Woods system, which was designed to liberate trade from the tentacles which had strangled it in the 1930s. Here the chief pressure came from the free-traders in Roosevelt's entourage, particularly Cordell Hull, US secretary of state from 1933 to 1944. The American free-traders believed that autarkic policies had led to the war; they also looked to the expansion of foreign markets to relieve collectivist pressures at home. In return for Lend-Lease, Britain was forced to pledge itself – in Article VII of the Lend-Lease Agreement of 1942 – to abandon trade discrimination after the war. Victory in war would also force Germany, Italy and Japan to abandon their autarkic systems. Between 1942 and 1944 Keynes, representing the British Treasury, and Harry Dexter White, the assistant secretary of the US Treasury, negotiated a set of institutions and rules designed to bring about a progressive liberalization of trade and payments by ensuring that a restored gold-exchange-rate system did not operate in a deflationary way. The Bretton Woods Agreement of 1944 set up an International Monetary Fund to supervise a system of fixed but adjustable exchange rates and to provide an adjustment facility to enable countries to finance temporary balance-of-payments deficits, and an International

Bank for Reconstruction and Development (the World Bank, as it was known) to provide economic aid to developing countries. To these was added, in 1947, a negotiating framework for freeing up trade – the General Agreement on Tariffs and Trade (GATT). These institutions can all be regarded as public goods of a free international order. The conception of the IMF, in particular, is that of a mutual-assurance scheme. The spirit with which Keynes approached the postwar world is eloquently conveyed in the last major speech of his life:

The separate economic blocs and all the friction and loss of friendship they must bring with them are expedients to which one may be driven in a hostile world . . . But it is surely crazy to prefer that. Above all, this determination to make trade truly international and to avoid the establishment of economic blocs which limit and restrict commercial intercourse outside them, is plainly an essential condition of the world's best hope, an Anglo-American understanding . . .[4]

The most powerful social invention of postwar liberalism was the welfare state. Its roots, of course, go back to the nineteenth century, when the state's duty to the deserving poor was first reaffirmed for an industrial economy. Bismarck's social-insurance scheme in Germany dates from 1883. But the welfare state achieved its classic philosophic and administrative expression in the Beveridge Report of 1942. William Beveridge addressed himself to another 'gap' in the *laissez-faire* system: the failure in the market for voluntary insurance against the contingency of 'interrupted earnings'. The core of the Beveridge concept was the notion of social insurance. All individuals would make flat-rate cash contributions to a National Insurance Fund which would provide flat-rate cash benefits for 'all the principal forms of cessation of earnings – unemployment, disability, retirements'. Although the principle of the flat-rate contribution implied a redistribution from low-risk to high-risk members of the Fund – that is why social insurance differed from private insurance – redistribution was not its aim.[5] In addition, Beveridge proposed a safety net of means-tested national assistance for those who fell 'out of benefit'. Other social services like public housing and health care were outside the Beveridge remit, though these today are considered part of the 'welfare state'. Three of Beveridge's assumptions are worth noticing: first, that poverty is a measurable absolute property such that one can work out a 'national minimum' required to abolish it; secondly, that the contingencies justifying compulsory *social* insurance (e.g. unemployment) are created by modern life rather than by individual fecklessness; thirdly, that the cost to society of social insurance and means-tested benefits will vary inversely with the level of employment. In other words, Beveridge looked to Keynes to keep the National Insurance Fund in balance at a socially acceptable level of contributions and benefits.

The third important contribution to anti-collectivist thought comes from a number of thinkers from Central Europe. All of them had personally experienced the disintegration of the nineteenth-century liberal order. If any single position unites them, it is their commitment to methodological individualism in the social sciences, with a consequent rejection of organic and idealist theories of the state. The German neo-liberals – men like Alfred Müller-Armack and Wilhelm Röpke – were, and remain, almost unknown in the Anglo-Saxon world, but their ideas inspired the West German conception of the 'social market economy' which flowered in the 1950s before degenerating into corporatism. The theses which commanded most general attention were those of the Austrians Karl Popper, Joseph Schumpeter, and Friedrich Hayek. Popper was a philosopher of science, Schumpeter and Hayek were economists; but all three stood aside from their scientific work to make political statements which nevertheless flowed from their scientific outlook.

In his books *The Open Society and Its Enemies* (1945) and *The Poverty of Historicism* (first published as articles in 1937), Popper launched a devastating attack on the scientific pretensions of collectivism. As he saw it, the intellectual tap root of totalitarianism was the unjustified claim of the social sciences to understand the laws of social development. In Popper's account, the ability of the speculative intellect to discern far-reaching patterns and laws in the jumble of events is its greatest glory and curse. Against its almost limitless powers of prophecy Popper opposes the method of the natural sciences, based on the production of falsifiable hypotheses, which he argues should also be the method of the social sciences. Of any valid scientific proposition it should be possible to ask, What kind of evidence would refute it? No large-scale social theory can pass the test.

Historicism is the claim to make predictions based on knowledge of social 'laws'. These predictions give a warrant for planning society to fit the laws. Marxism was the main example Popper had in mind. He rejected such teleological theories in favour of the view that the future is open, follows no predetermined path. The future depends on how we behave; politics is, to a large extent, the master of circumstances. Popper denied that we can ever have the knowledge to undertake 'holistic' planning. Attempts to remodel societies end with planners being driven to transform human nature to fit their plans rather than adapting their plans to fit human beings. In place of holistic planning Popper advocated 'piecemeal social engineering' based on testable sociological or economic propositions. The piecemeal reformer must start with individual purposes. He may have larger ends, but he proceeds by tinkering, conscious of how little he knows, in the manner of the experimental scientist.

Schumpeter's attack was aimed at the 'Italian school' of early-twentieth-century anti-democratic theorists – Pareto, Gaetano Mosca and Robert Michels – who purported to show that democracy was bound to be a sham. In his *Capitalism, Socialism and Democracy* (1942) Schumpeter set out to provide a realistic theory of democracy. He agreed with the anti-democrats that the common good cannot be discerned by the counting of heads. But the anti-democratic argument for despotism is no more valid than the anti-market argument for collectivism.

Schumpeter claimed that the superior rationality of enlightened minorities could prevail within a system of formal democracy. Democracy should be understood as a particular type of method for producing a government, by means of a competitive struggle by political parties for people's votes. This theory has the advantage of placing the emphasis on leadership as the vital factor in choosing and articulating issues, and in mobilizing support for policy, while ensuring that the leaders are sufficiently accountable to the led, through the competitive process itself, to prevent political monopoly. His model of democracy is explicitly an imperfect-competition model borrowed from economics. Enlightened minority rule can be reconciled with accountability, provided that 'the effective range of political decision [does] not extend too far'.

The ideas of Keynes, Beveridge, Popper and Schumpeter provide mutually supporting arguments for limited interventionism. Keynes's 'managed capitalism' requires exactly the kind of enlightened minority rule promised by Schumpeter. Beveridge's social-insurance principle, building on the model of private insurance, is an example of the 'piecemeal' interventionism favoured by Popper. The operational principle which emerges from all this is that a flourishing liberal market economy needs to be underpinned by compensatory finance and social insurance, which can be safely entrusted to democratic government.

Hayek stands somewhat apart from this postwar liberal consensus by virtue of the intransigence of his commitment to the market economy. His *The Road to Serfdom* (1944) was, at one level, a culmination of the Austrian school's attack on the logic of central planning. The early socialist justification of a state-owned planning system was that it would actually achieve the efficient allocation of resources which the market system promised but failed to deliver. It would do so by eliminating the 'waste' associated with capitalist consumption, booms and slumps, monopoly profits, etc. No more would the captain of industry 'eat an unwholesome dinner on which ten times as much labour has been expended as on the meat by which his labourers maintain their health' nor would his wife 'crowd his house with indiscriminate articles of furniture and ornamentation which have no merit beyond the amount of labour that has been wasted on them'.[6]

Enrico Barone (1908) and Ludwig von Mises (1920) had argued that efficient Communism was an impossible dream because if all capital were publicly owned there would be no market for capital goods in terms of which competing investment projects could be properly costed. 'Instead of the economy of "anarchical" production the senseless order of an irrational machine would be supreme.'[7] Hayek (1935) argued that the planning authority lacked the information to solve the vast number of equations needed to coordinate the demand and supply of millions of products.[8] The culmination of this critique was that in any centrally planned system the arbitrary preferences of the central planners were bound to replace the wants of rational consumers, leading to much greater waste and inefficiency in production than anything resulting from the 'anarchy of the market'.

Apologists for Stalin like the Cambridge economist Maurice Dobb (1933) conceded that the object of planning was to replace spontaneous market forces by the centre's priorities, but argued that these would be determined by the 'general social advantage'. The difficulties of central planning had been greatly exaggerated. Equalization of incomes would allow the production of standardized consumption goods. The central planning board's task was to choose between a few technological alternatives. Dobb's defence evaded the problem of the rationality of planning by positing a single aim, as in war: in this case industrialization. It was for this purpose that the planning movement was taken up in the developing countries. But the connection between industrialization and welfare was left unexamined. Hayek ironically commended Dobb for his 'very courageous step' in asserting that life under socialism 'would be like life in a barracks'.[9]

In *The Road to Serfdom*, Hayek broadened the argument. It is an illusion, he said, that you can have democratic planning – central planning minus Stalin. The crux of his argument was that centrally determined ends can be achieved only by coercion. This is for two main reasons. First, outside wartime or temporary enthusiasm, there is never sufficient voluntary consent for the goals of the central plan. Planning curtails freedom; resistance develops, which has to be met by increased coercion. Hence the inexorable tendency for democratic planning to become totalitarian planning. International planning, however pacific it sounds, is in fact fatal to peace, since it requires interferences with the movement of people and goods, and the increasing use of compulsion as spatial extension reduces the degree of consent: it is 'one of the most fatal illusions' to believe that substituting state-bargaining for competition for markets or raw materials reduces international friction. Secondly, partial planning creates problems which, to the planner, appear soluble only by more extensive planning. 'Once the free working of the market is impeded beyond a certain degree, the planner will be forced to extend his controls until they become all-comprehensive.'[10] If, for example, the government plans income distribution for the sake of social justice, it cannot refuse responsibility for anyone's fate or position, and the question of the 'due station of different individuals and groups' becomes the 'central political problem'.[11] Thus Hayek saw 'corporativism' – a system in which 'competition is more or less suppressed but planning is left in the hands of the independent monopolies of the separate industries' – as a staging post to complete collectivism. Democratic socialism and 'corporativism' alike were delusions: their mounting problems leave as the only alternatives a return to competition or an extension of state control 'which, if it is to be made effective, must become progressively more complete and detailed'.[12]

Hayek believed that competition is the only way of allocating resources efficiently, because the knowledge needed to adjust supplies and demands in all markets is not available to central authority, but exists only in a dispersed system of prices. But he was careful not to identify economic liberalism with *laissez-faire* – a mistake made by liberal thinkers in the nineteenth century. A 'carefully thought out legal framework is necessary for competition to work beneficially'.[13] He distinguished between the rule of law and legality. To have a rule of the road is different from a policeman telling people where to go. The distinction is between formal rules which are intended to be merely 'instrumental in the pursuit of people's various individual ends' and substantive rules providing 'for the actual needs of people as they arise' and choosing 'deliberately between them'. Hayek's insistence that a beneficial market system requires a consciously contrived constitutional order is the most important Continental European contribution to the theory of economic liberalism. It underlay the neo-liberal idea of the 'social market economy', and influenced the construction of the European Community. Hayek himself thought that a world government would be needed to entrench economic liberalism internationally.

As Hayek saw it, the planning cult arises from the strata of scientists and engineers mistakenly supposing that science can settle matters of politics and morality. He made no distinction between Fascism and Communism: the 'coercive organisation of public life' was common to both. It was no accident that both had originated in Germany, a fact which he traced to the 'quite unique influence' of Germany's scientific and technical specialists on its political and social opinions. Apart from ideas, the impetus to collectivism came from great vested interests of organized capital and labour aiming for a corporative society. But Hayek also acknowledged that capitalist failure to provide security was an important source of collectivist feeling. Minimal indispensable security should be provided 'outside the market' for its victims. But he was suspicious of public spending: 'we shall have carefully to watch our set up if we are to avoid making all economic activity progressively more dependent on the direction and volume of government expenditure'.[14] Hayek placed more emphasis than did Keynes on trying to break up rigidities in product and labour markets which led to the fluctuations in employment and output rather than in relative prices and wages.

Keynes thought Hayek had damaged an extremely powerful case by overstatement. 'Morally and philosophically' he found himself in agreement with 'virtually the whole of it'. He made the practical point that to adopt Hayek's economic programme would 'only lead in practice to disillusion with the results of your philosophy'. Keynes argued that government support for full employment was part of the institutional order necessary to support economic liberalism, not a 'thin end of the wedge' leading to collectivism. Keynes claimed, against Hayek, that 'dangerous acts can be done safely in a community which thinks and feels rightly, which would be the way to hell if they were executed by those who think and feel wrongly'.[15] The question being begged here is precisely whether the community will continue to 'think and feel rightly' if dangerous acts become part of the expected order of things. To this Hayek had already given his answer: 'If we are determined not to allow unemployment at any price, and are not willing to use coercion, we shall be driven to . . . a general and considerable inflation.'[16] This was a remarkably accurate prediction of the dilemma which came to face Western governments in the 1970s.

The fuse lit by *The Road to Serfdom* was slow-burning. The book made a great splash when it appeared, but it faded from consciousness in the 1950s when the success of the 'mixed economy' of public and private sectors seemed to discredit its main thesis of the slippery slope to totalitarianism. In 1947 Hayek helped found the Mont Pelerin Society to provide a meeting ground for anti-collectivist economists. One of its first members was Milton Friedman from Chicago, a leader of the anti-collectivist revolt of the 1970s.

The main purpose of all five thinkers – Keynes, Beveridge, Popper, Schumpeter and Hayek – was to repel the intellectual claims of collectivism, particularly in its radical version of totalitarian planning. In this they succeeded. They created an optimistic climate of opinion, which in turn was an important cause of changed political and economic behaviour. However, as an explicit defence of a free society their performance was much more equivocal. Keynes allowed a wide degree of discretion to his central managers; Beveridge failed to reconcile his 'desire to protect individual freedom and responsibility' with 'the view of poverty as not being the responsibility of the individual'.[17] Popper was a social democrat; Schumpeter thought socialism was inevitable. Even Hayek's defence rested to an uncomfortable extent on the knowledge limitations of the central planner, rather than on an affirmation of the value of freedom. In short, their aim was to establish secure defences against collectivism after a half-century of retreat. In a sense what they did was to anaesthetize political discourse. One no longer needed to argue about socialism versus capitalism, struggle versus harmony, planning versus markets, equality versus liberty or efficiency, because ways had been found of finessing these contentious questions. Political debate could give way to a discussion of managerial technique. In 1960 the sociologist Daniel Bell proclaimed the 'end of ideology' and announced a 'rough consensus' of Western intellectuals behind the idea of a managed welfare-capitalism. Political theory almost disappeared during the 1950s and 1960s, to be replaced by political science: the positivist study of political institutions. Debate almost ceased in economics, too. The collectivist creep which started again in the 1960s, as Hayek predicted it would, could be presented as an extension of existing state activity, with no contentious, or overly contentious, implications. It was only belatedly realized that one of the biggest 'gaps' in *laissez-faire* remained unclosed: the constitution of liberty itself.

The era which ended sometime in the 1970s has been called 'the Keynesian age'. This is a bit of Anglo-Saxon presumption: Keynesian policy was never central except to the managers of the British and American economies, and even in the United States only from the 1960s onwards; elsewhere it was added to a portfolio of policies. Nevertheless, there is some truth in the characterization, since Anglo-American attitudes and policies played a predominant role in shaping the environment in which national economies worked. The economics profession was largely Anglo-American, or trained in Britain and the United States. Outside Sweden, there was very little home-grown economics in Europe. The Austrian school had no influence in Austria; its members had all left anyway. In the developing countries economic doctrines were imported from America and Britain, together with capital and know-how: socialism was Britain's main postwar export to India. This situation continues today, with the economic life of the post-Communist countries being reshaped by Harvard, Chicago and the Massachusetts Institute of Technology.

The basic Keynesian policy model did not change much between the 1940s and 1970s; but Keynesianism was not institutionally static. Once it emerged from its heavy encrustation of wartime controls in the early 1950s, one can discern three distinct phases: managerial, planning, corporatist. Each additional layer was added as performance deteriorated. The first phase, which came out of the cooperation of British and American élites in the Second World War, was the least interventionist. This period, which lasted from 1950 to 1964, can be called the Keynesian 'golden age'. The Keynesian guarantee of full employment was a background factor to private business decisions; it did not have to be invoked by active government policy. The second phase, which lasted from 1964 to 1974, was heavily influenced by fears of slow growth and the successes of Soviet planning. The third phase, which overlapped with the second, lasted till 1979–80. Its unique feature was the attempt to control incomes.

Broadly speaking, the twenty years from 1950 to 1970 were the twentieth-century equivalent to the mid-nineteenth-century 'age of equipoise', in which the governing ideas and facts conspired to produce a long virtually uninterrupted boom. By historical standards, unemployment was exceptionally low, growth in real incomes exceptionally fast, economies exceptionally stable; all were achieved at a very modest cost in inflation. The political economies of Western nations were only mildly collectivist, with the government share of taxes and spending in GNP not much in excess of 30 per cent.

This achievement resulted from a happy conjuncture of forces. Across the developed world there were 'widespread opportunities to imitate American technology, to contract low productivity agriculture, and to exploit cheap energy'.[18] Opportunities for technological catch-up with the United States gave capital a high marginal productivity, leading to high investment demand. A high rate of productivity growth allowed a sufficient rise in real incomes to satisfy workers' aspirations while keeping unit costs fairly stable. The economist Walt Rostow has hypothesized that policy or institutions had little to do with this: the industrial world was enjoying the downswing of a fourth Kondratieff cycle based on cheap food, raw materials and energy.[19]* However, the Kondratieff cycles are price cycles. They presuppose the existence of a relatively liberal global market economy, and policy and institutions did play an important part in the revival of such an economy after the war.

A key role was played by the United States, as macroeconomic 'manager' and security guarantor of the free world. During the 'golden age' proper, only the United States enjoyed the luxury of an 'autonomous' macroeconomic policy. Under the gold-exchange standard set up at Bretton Woods, the United States was on the gold standard, other countries held most of their reserves in dollars. Monetary conditions for the system as a whole were set by US financial policy. Under presidents Truman and Eisenhower, US budgetary policy was conservative, interest rates were low, the balance of trade was in surplus. Till the mid-1960s, the United States provided most countries with a reasonably secure anti-inflationary anchor, while supplying them with enough liquidity to prevent the deflationary contractions associated with the pre-war gold standard. The stability of the monetary regime allowed a progressive liberalization of a multilateral payments and trading system which, as Adam Smith would have predicted, was highly favourable to the growth of real incomes. The long boom did not depend on Keynesian fiscal policy – countries running budget deficits. However, the explicit or implicit commitment by governments

---

* Nikolai Kondratieff (1892–1931), a Russian statistician, suggested that capitalist economies experience long cycles, lasting forty or fifty years.

to avoid economic collapse – and, just as important, the belief that they knew how to – contributed importantly to the state of confidence necessary to sustain the private investment boom for so long. In short, it was the *Pax Americana* which secured a rough and ready macroeconomic balance across the 'free world' during the golden age, much as the *Pax Britannica* had done in the nineteenth century. The existence of a buoyant international economy (unlike in the 1930s) in turn made national economic problems much more tractable.

However, towards the end of the 1950s there occurred one of those shifts of mood which was to wreck this mid-century version of Keynes's 'economic Eldorado'. The intellectual consensus turned collectivist again. Socialism was refloated on the back of Keynesian economics, welfare expenditures and planning for 'faster growth'. Capitalism was once more found wanting. It was not achieving prosperity as fast as was technically possible. It was not delivering as much quality as was desirable. The conviction that capitalism had solved its problems was succeeded by the deepest gloom about its prospects. Once more the old maxims of collectivism were pressed into service. And once more they helped create a world of facts which favoured an extension of collectivist practices.

To explain the shift of mood, one has to remember that the socialist intelligentsia in Europe and the United States, while sufficiently inoculated against Stalinism, had never accepted the achieved 'equipoise' of the 1950s as something to be preserved as a good in itself. In fact the 'affluent society' which capitalism created in the 1950s was rightly interpreted as a defeat for classic socialism. They were therefore disposed to magnify its problems in order to justify collectivist interventions to improve its working. It only needed the Soviet Union's *economic* success under Khrushchev to fan the dying embers of socialism into life. The new collectivism focused on two issues: growth and public spending.

Growthmanship had its roots in three historically specific obsessions: the fear of the United States that it was 'losing ground' to the Soviet Union; the fear of Britain that it was losing out to the faster-growing Germans and French; and the perceived need of developing countries to 'catch up' with the West. The general stimulus to Western growthmanship came from the feeling that the main sources of postwar market-led growth were drying up. Stagnation would endanger the fragile legitimacy of 'welfare capitalism', which depended on annual additions to welfare spending. Higher spending on the social services required continually expanding state revenue, which, given the limits of tax tolerance, required continual growth, if inflation was to be avoided.

The main change in the 1960s was that most Western governments started to 'target' annual growth rates. This entailed 'planning for growth', though of an indicative kind. Planning became almost bipartisan in the 1960s, but its strongest appeal was to the Left, which discovered, or rediscovered, important 'lessons' to be drawn from the 'successes' of Soviet planning. The British Labour leader Harold Wilson, who became prime minister in 1964, returned from trips to Russia and China in 1957 'with his faith in the efficacy of the command economies of East Europe and China further reinforced . . . References to supposed Soviet economic success, and the moral to be drawn from it for the United Kingdom, spiced many of his speeches before the 1959 election.'[20] Wilson's favourite economist, Thomas Balogh, predicted that the USSR would overtake British and US output per head within a few years. Wilson's lieutenant, Richard Crossman, expounded the same view as part of his 're-thinking of socialism' in 1957. Crossman pointed out that Keynes had solved the unemployment problem but not the wastefulness of capitalism. He was impressed by 'the terrifying contrast between the drive and missionary energy displayed by the Communist bloc and the lethargic, comfortable indolence of the Western democracies . . . Judged in terms of national security, scientific and technological development, popular education, and, finally, even of mass living standards, free enterprise is losing out in the peaceful competition between East and West.'[21]

Right through the 'golden age', planning doctrines had retained a powerful attraction for developing countries. The Latin American experience during the Great Depression, when the prices of food and primary products had collapsed disastrously, had led to the widespread adoption of the Soviet strategy of 'catching up' with the West through industrialization. 'Industrialization rather than agriculture', proclaimed Kwame Nkrumah, Ghana's post-independence leader, 'is the means by which rapid improvement in African living standards is possible.' Between 1940 and 1965, seventy of the ninety poor and middle-income countries published one or more development plans. The 'development economics' which rationalized them was a mixture of neo-Marxist explanations of 'underdevelopment', 'infant-industry' arguments derived from Friedrich List, and neo-Keynesian growth models. A key idea was that the integration of poor countries into the world capitalist system had destroyed viable artisan industries, creating rural underemployment, while turning the terms of trade against commodity exporters, who sold their products at fluctuating market prices while manufactured goods sold at administered prices. Neo-Keynesian growth theory held that the rate of growth of economies depended on the rate of growth of physical investment. Western economic advisers 'emphasized setting national targets for growth and investment and using governmental authority to achieve those targets'.[22]

Growth strategies of this kind relied on overvalued exchange rates to check traditional exports and cheapen the cost of importing capital equipment, on import quotas to create uncontested domestic markets for 'infant industries', on import licences to limit entry to necessary capital goods, on price controls to offset quotas, on taxes on agriculture to pay for subsidies to industry, on directed credit and subsidized interest rates to allocate investment funds, on public ownership of the industrial sector, and so on. The idea of 'victimhood' was a powerful help in extracting aid from the West. A succession of Indian five-year plans aimed at creating an industrial sector with forward and backward linkages. The economist Peter Bauer pointed out the absurdity of governments taking on such ambitious tasks when they were unable to fulfil 'even the elementary and necessary functions of government'.[23] Such warnings were ignored.

In the 1960s the public sector started to play a much larger part in the thinking of Western leaders and their advisers than it had in the 1950s. Their basic idea seems to have been that a planned growth in output required a complementary expansion of the public sector to ensure both the requisite supply of skills and technology and the requisite level of demand. The key tool was investment: investment in people (education, training, research) and investment in physical plant (schools, hospitals, houses). By causing the national income to grow faster than it otherwise would, public investment would generate the saving necessary to finance it. However, such a strategy also fitted the socialist preference for collective over individual consumption. That an increase in collective consumption was bound to increase the numbers and power of officials was not seen as a major problem.

A final factor in the pro-collectivist mood of the 1960s was the popularity of the theory of 'convergence' among Western (and also Eastern) social scientists. In essence, they believed that the technology associated with large-scale business organization would force all societies which used it towards indicative planning. Thus the Soviet Union would liberalize its over-rigid central planning system, the West would socialize its private planning systems, and 'only one thing seems certain, the convergence of the evolutions of East and West towards democratic socialism'.[24] These arguments, as we have seen, hark back to the late nineteenth century. They reflect the same fascination with concentrated private power and the need to 'control it in the public interest', the same assumed relationship between efficiency and large-scale production, the same belief that large corporations 'control' their suppliers and markets, the same assumption of standardized consumer wants, and the same inability to imagine technological change. Detroit and Sverdlovsk, said Galbraith, one of the leading convergers, were twin expressions of a common engineering culture which would force the development of matching political forms. His most influential book, *The Affluent Society* (1958), with its evocative imagery of 'private affluence and public squalor', argued that 'social balance' required a big increase in public investment in human capital, transport systems, housing, etc. The popularity of the book was largely due 'to the climate of debate [in the USA] on the national purpose and on the trade-off between private enterprise and social responsibility . . . which resulted from the launching of the first Sputnik in 1957'.[25]

Expectation that the rate of capital accumulation would fall was not unreasonable after postwar reconstruction and exploitation of existing technology had run their course. Much more questionable was the extension of Keynes's thinking from the short-run problem of securing full use of existing resources to the problem of securing the 'optimal' growth of these resources. It is now realized that concepts like the 'optimal' or 'warranted' rate of growth have no concrete meaning. A society's potential resources are simply the sum of the things people want (including future goods) together with the efforts they are willing to make to discover and produce them. No one knows how to make societies grow faster. The only safe rule is to create an environment in which enterprise can flourish.

This is not what politicians generally want to hear: certainly they did not in the 1960s. They wanted faster growth because it would get them elected or solve their problems. The economists promised them Faustian achievements. Their faith was built on theory and computerized forecasting. The causes of slow growth were unproblematic: slow-growing economies were not investing enough in new productive capacity. Computerized growth models could tell the planners where to put in the investments needed to realize the overall growth plan. By the late 1960s the British Treasury model of the economy 'contained six hundred equations and required two hundred exogenous assumptions and no single person could understand how it was all supposed to work'.[26] Together, economic theory and the computer could give a community 'full employment . . . at a rate of capital formation it wants, and can accomplish all this . . . with the degree of income distribution it desires' – thus said Paul Samuelson, doyen of American economists.[27] He did not add, though he certainly believed, that this could all be done at the rate of inflation 'it' wanted. Samuelson would have been horrified at the suggestion that only a coerced economy could even attempt these things.

American Keynesian economists detected a growing 'output gap' – a gap between the actual annual growth of output of the American economy and what it could produce – which they attributed to 'fiscal drag' – the tendency, with the existing tax structure, for public revenues to rise faster than public expenditure as private incomes increased. At full employment there would be a budget surplus of $10 billion, available to 'finance the Federal programmes needed to accelerate the growth of productive capacity and meet national priorities at home and abroad'.[28] British Keynesians argued that investment in Britain was being held back by 'stop-go' policies to protect the balance of payments. State-led investment policies would put the economy on to a higher-growth path which would ease the balance-of-payments constraint by promoting a faster rate of export growth. The key assumption in these neo-Keynesian growth models was that growth in productivity would match growth in investment, owing to the effect of dynamic economies of scale. Thus full employment was no barrier to demand-led expansion: growth, in the jargon, was demand- not supply-constrained.

It all turned out to be a miasma. In the British five-year plan of 1965, 'indicated' growth rates were worked out for each sector over a five-year period. Against a background of rapidly rising public spending, supply was to be geared up by a battery of microeconomic interventions supervised and coordinated by a Department of Economic Affairs, sectoral planning agencies and an Industrial Reorganization Corporation. Import surcharges, export subsidies, standardization of output, rationalization of output, mergers, public share acquisition in companies, investment grants, licences, a selective employment tax, prices and wages policies were the order of the day. A complete planning system was established – on paper. In fact most of it was soon scrapped in the face of rising inflation and balance-of-payments crises. The one bit of the economy which went on growing was public spending: up from 38 per cent of GNP in 1964 to 49.3 per cent in 1974 (including transfer payments, but excluding spending on financial assets).[29] From the 1960s the share of public spending in national income started rising everywhere. Total government outlays in the OECD countries (including transfer payments) rose from 36.7 per cent in 1960–68 to 41.2 per cent in 1968–73 to 48.5 per cent in 1973–9. This association of Keynesianism with increasing public spending was to prove fateful.

From the global point of view, the most significant macro-economic episode was the Kennedy–Johnson tax cut and 'Great Society' spending programmes of 1964–6. These, together with the inflationary financing of the Vietnam War, ended the United States' role as the world's anti-inflationary anchor. Synchronized policy-induced booms in the early 1970s destroyed the Bretton Woods system of fixed exchange rates and triggered off a commodity-price explosion which culminated in a quadrupling of the price of crude oil in 1973–4. Between 1968 and 1973 a new phenomenon, 'stagflation', appeared. It was taking continually more unemployment to check the rise in prices, and continually more inflation to check the rise in unemployment. For the OECD countries as a whole the 'misery index' (inflation plus unemployment) rose from 6.2 per cent in 1960–68 to 9.3 per cent in 1968–73 to 15.6 per cent in 1973–9.

With the worsening of macroeconomic performance, the Hayekian logic asserted itself. In *The Road to Serfdom* Hayek had predicted that, 'once the working of the market is impeded beyond a certain degree, the planner will be forced to extend his controls'; specifically, as we have seen, he had warned that 'If we are determined not to allow unemployment at any price, and are not willing to use coercion, we shall be driven to . . . a general and considerable inflation.' The earliest response of most Western governments to the rising 'misery index' was not to abandon deficit finance, but to buttress it with 'additional instruments'. As an alternative to a 'socially intolerable' level of unemployment, an administered 'incomes policy', covering both the general wage level and relative wages, was needed to keep average wage growth throughout the economy in line with average productivity growth. Such a policy would be administered and policed by business and trade-union organizations. Controls on wages might be made acceptable to wage-earners by higher taxes on profits and dividends, a compensating 'social wage', subsidies to 'essential' industries, improved workplace protection, and pro-union legislation. Such policies were tried in various forms in all industrial countries right through the 1970s. Social scientists started to talk about the 'coming corporatism'. Of such policies, Alan Coddington commented with considerable justice, 'given enough buttressing [with 'additional instruments'] anything can be achieved: if the central government authorities are in a position to write a script for the whole economic drama, then they can make sure that it conforms to their prevailing idea of an edifying overall plot, and one in which the supporting characters never have a chance to upstage the stars'. That 'the degree of centralisation of economic power is allowed to emerge as a residual to the solution of the problems of macroeconomic management' is precisely what Hayek predicted would happen.[30] A socialist economist concluded that the necessary conditions of a permanent incomes policy would be 'price control, steady growth of real incomes, full employment, a proletarian government and a non-permissive approach to breaches in labour discipline'.[31] In practice, the amount of consent for incomes policies was never enough to make them work well for long; democratic governments shrank from increasing the level of coercion needed to make them work, and just pumped more money into their stagnating economies. Western societies, in another phrase of the day, were becoming 'ungovernable'.

What compounded the problems of all governments in the 1970s was the slowdown in the rate of productivity growth. The dash for growth had precisely the opposite effect from what was intended. The OECD rate of growth of real GDP per capita (a reasonable proxy for productivity growth when there is little change in the size of the labour force) fell from 3.9 per cent in 1960–68 to 3.5 per cent in 1968–73 to 1.9 per cent in 1973–9. For this there were plausible technological and social explanations, but the most convincing reason was the distortions to the supply side of the economy caused by taxes, regulations and subsidies, by restriction of competition, by the mounting costs to employers of hiring and firing workers, and by a misaligned capital structure tied to government orders. An important consequence of the growth slowdown was the so-called 'fiscal crisis' of the state, as welfare expenditures, driven by the explosion of entitlements in the 1960s, went on expanding in line with projected growth rates which were not realized.

Eventually Western governments had had enough. In the face of the second oil price rise, in 1979–80, they tightened fiscal and monetary policy, bringing about the worst slump since the 1930s. Developing countries, which had maintained their public investment booms throughout the 1970s by borrowing recycled petrodollars at negative real interest rates, found themselves faced with crippling debt burdens as export earnings collapsed, real interest rates rose to punitive levels, and foreign investment dried up.

While this was going on, no one paid much attention to the command economies, which had also shared to some extent in the petrodollar bonanza. What no one suspected was that the diseases which forced a change in direction of political economy in the 'free' world were about to terminate Communism.

CHAPTER SIX

WHY DID SOVIET COMMUNISM COLLAPSE?

Like all empires, the Soviet Empire was based on coercion, and broke up when it lost the will and means to coerce its subjects. However, while the collapse of the colonial empires of this century left their economic systems intact, the collapse of Soviet rule brought down the Soviet economy too. The Cold War ended in a double victory for the West: the end of Russia as a superpower, and the end of Communism as a challenge to capitalism. This is because Soviet Communism was a system of economic as well as political monopoly. Not only did the Communist Party control the state, it also owned and directed the economy. The Soviet economy could not function were it not centrally commanded, for it existed to fulfil a central plan, not to satisfy market demand. When Communist Party rule collapsed, the central planning system collapsed. When the central planning system collapsed, the economy collapsed. There was no one to tell it what to do.

There has been nothing quite like the Communist system in human history, either in its ambitions or in the scale of its penetration into the lives of its subjects. The Soviet economy was a giant state factory, churning out goods in the amounts and proportions decided by its director. It had to have enough coal to produce steel, and enough steel to produce plants, and enough plants to produce tractors, and enough tractors to produce food, and enough food to produce workers, and enough workers to produce coal, and so on. What human purposes this factory was meant to serve was not, in the end, a question to which an honest answer could be given. One could not reply, as in the West, 'What is produced is what the people wish to have,' because the wishes of the people were not allowed to determine what the factory produced, either through the voting system or through purchases in the market-place. But it is evident that once a deficit of production develops in any important sector – because either of plan underfulfilment or plan mistake – the whole factory starts to seize up. This is essentially what happened once the coercion which tied component activities to plan fulfilment was lightened.

The proximate cause of the collapse of the Soviet Empire was state bankruptcy. This is the common cause of the breakdown of all rule from the Roman Empire to our own day. The economy declines, while the state's need for revenue expands. A parallel – suggestive rather than exact – is the process by which imperial Rome became feudal Europe. As in Roman times, the Soviet economy was based on 'extensive' production, and started to decay when it ran out of free, or cheap, resources of land and labour. Like the Roman state, the Soviet state lost to its territorial magnates its ability to appropriate a declining surplus. In both cases the decline in state revenue was matched by growing pressure on the state's social and military budget: the growing cost of 'bread and circuses' and of countering barbarian pressure on the frontiers in Roman times had its counterparts in growing subsidies to loss-making industries and the cost of countering Reagan's arms build-up in the 1980s. Both empires split up into a large number of successor states when their central governments ran out of money. As Montesquieu wrote of Rome, 'the empire was thrown into such a condition that, not being able to subsist without soldiers, it could not subsist with them'. Repeated attempts to reconstitute the Roman imperium failed, as it proved impossible to recentralize sufficient revenues to do the job. Similarly, the prospect today is not for a reassertion of Soviet might, but a further unravelling of Russia and the Soviet Union's successor states. Whether from the ashes of the Soviet empire will arise the liberalism of a limited state and a market economy or a congeries of warring nationalities is the great unresolved problem of the 'transformation'.

The collapse of the Soviet system was brought about by one

of the most interesting leaders of our century – Mikhail Gorbachev, general secretary of the Communist Party and, for two years, president of the Soviet Union. Through the fog of his delphic oratory and his contradictory zigzagging actions, it is difficult to understand what he thought he was doing. Clearly, he did not aim for the breakup of the Soviet state or the breakdown of the 'socialist mode of production'. He was a Communist, indeed a Leninist, whose main aim was to preserve and strengthen Soviet power. He did not lack ruthlessness. Most of what he did, or attempted, had its roots in previous efforts to galvanize a decaying system. The crunch came in 1990–91, when it was apparent that the reforms were not working and that the Soviet Empire was in deep crisis.

All the evidence suggests that this failure astounded Gorbachev. As the revolt against Soviet rule gathered pace, not just in Eastern Europe but in the Soviet Union itself, he seemed to have two choices: to put himself at the head of the democratic forces or try to reimpose a Communist Party military dictatorship. He was lucid and intelligent enough to realize that neither alternative was open to *him*. He was a master of bureaucratic politics, of balancing different factions against each other. His power rested on being indispensable both to the reformers and to the hardliners, each group seeing him as a guarantee against the victory of the other. By the end of 1990 at the latest, Gorbachev had come to the end of that game. With the system of Communist rule collapsing all round him, he was seen as an obstacle to both reform and reaction, and his days as powerbroker were numbered. The only people for whom he was now indispensable were the Western leaders, for whom he guaranteed an orderly waning of Soviet power. By a supreme irony Gorbachev at the moment of his fall was canonized outside the Soviet Union for having brought about a result entirely contrary to his intention – Western victory in the Cold War.

What the Hungarian economist János Kornai called the 'classical socialist system' is characterized by the political monopoly

of the Communist Party and its ideology, by state ownership
of the means of production, by bureaucratic coordination of
production, and by the system of incentives – including terror
– which makes the system work. Kornai argues that everything
more or less follows from the seizure of power by a revolutionary party imbued with a Communist ideology. 'It is not the
property form – state ownership – that erects the political structure of classical socialism over itself. Quite the reverse: the
given political structure brings about the property form it
deems desirable . . . The further elimination of private ownership is taken, the more consistently can full subjection be
imposed.'[1] State ownership made possible imperative planning;
imperative planning secured the subjection of the economy and
society to the wishes of the party. From the time of Stalin's
ascendancy in the late 1920s, party leadership and state government were merged in a supreme body, the Politburo, headed
by the general secretary of the Communist Party, while all governmental and managerial appointments lower down the
command chain were reserved for party members – the
nomenklatura.

Imperative planning (what Kornai calls 'bureaucratic coordination', otherwise the 'command economy') lay at the heart
of 'classical socialism'. Into one end of the giant factory went
inputs of labour, raw materials, electric power, etc. These produced semi-finished or capital goods, which eventually ground
out consumer goods at the other end: tanks for the state; shoes
for the people. Attached to the giant factory was a giant collective farm, operated on the same principles, whose job was to
feed the factory's population. Of the inputs into the system,
labour was allocated by a mixture of market and non-market
mechanisms: wage and amenity differentials were designed to
influence the flow of labour from rural to urban areas, and into
the desired sectors; non-market allocation at various times consisted of forced labour camps (slavery), work books held by the
enterprise manager without which a worker could not get another job, the passport system controlling internal movement,
allocation of training places, and the 'one-enterprise' towns

which bound a population to a single employer. These administrative mechanisms reflected Kautsky's dictum that 'socialist
production is irreconcilable . . . with the [worker's] freedom to
work when, where and how he wills'.[2] There was consumer
choice, though not sovereignty, in the sense that individuals
were free to choose between goods supplied by the planners to
the state stores, but production was not changed in response to
shortages or surpluses.

Typically, plans of various durations for the whole economy
were drawn up by Gosplan, the state planning commission.
These were designed to implement the strategic targets set by
the Politburo for the growth of the economy and its division
into capital, consumer and military goods and the thousands of
different types of these goods. Gosplan worked out the 'material balances' – the inputs of labour and materials necessary to
achieve the targeted outputs – over the whole economy and for
each sector; the sectoral or branch ministries told each enterprise in its sector how much to produce, from whom to buy its
inputs, to whom to sell its output, and at what prices, and what
technology to use. The Soviet state deliberately fostered monopolies and gigantomania in order to coordinate production:
73 per cent of enterprises had over 1,000 employees. There was
much bargaining between Gosplan, the branch ministries and
the enterprises before final plans were agreed. Prices were passive – book-keeping transactions between firms, and between
firms and the state. They did not determine what was produced
but were grafted on to the plan for accounting and monitoring
purposes ('rouble control') and to subsidise some kinds of consumption and prevent others. Over a succession of plans the
party-state could determine the rate of investment and its
allocation to various sectors, the division of consumption between collective and individual, and the shares of different
goods in current output in line with its preferred structure of
income distribution.

What was it all for? The earliest justification of this kind of
state-owned planning system was that it would eliminate the
injustice and waste associated with a capitalist market economy.

The charter premiss of socialism is moral: because capital is created by labour, the price paid to owners of capital (including land) for its use is seen as a subtraction from the value created by workers. The income distribution produced by a privately owned economy is therefore morally unjust. This injustice gives rise to a particular form of waste, as resources which could be used to improve mass living conditions are appropriated by an exploiting minority and frittered away in parasitical consumption. Injustice and waste can both be eliminated by transferring ownership of the productive instruments to the state and planning for need rather than profit. The advantages of such a system over capitalism will lie in the elimination of monopoly profits, the elimination of the waste caused by slumps and unemployment, and a more equal income distribution.

These formulations left room for much divergence about the central justification of planning. Was it to be considered a way of perfecting the market system – i.e. of achieving its promised efficiency in allocation minus its distributional and other imperfections – or a method of imposing a different scale of values on society from those dictated by free consumer choice?

This theoretical debate went on right through the life of the Soviet system. As we have seen, Mises and Hayek argued that it was impossible for a centrally planned system to mimic the market. To counter this, Oscar Lange and A. P. Lerner (1936–7) said that the planning authority could cause state-owned firms to react appropriately to simulated market signals. The planning authority would require all firms to minimize their average costs per unit of output and to fix that scale of output at which marginal cost equals product price, and would then announce starting prices, like an auctioneer. Shortages and surpluses of goods at the initial set of prices would then indicate to the planning authority the need to raise the prices of goods and services in short supply, and to lower those in excess supply, allowing it to obtain, by a method of trial and error, an equilibrium price structure – one that clears all markets. Hayek attacked such proposals as Utopian: 'To imagine that all this adjustment could be brought about by successive orders by the central authority when the necessity is noticed, and that then every price is fixed and changed until some degree of equilibrium is obtained is certainly an absurd idea.'[3]

Stalin was not interested in mimicking the market. Both Communist theory and the strategic ambitions of the regime demanded that industrial development should take place as rapidly as possible. To this end, Stalin closed down the relatively free economy of the New Economic Policy and confiscated the nation's total capital stock. Initially this was simply its industry. His next move was to confiscate the larger prize: the wealth of the countryside – land, livestock and labour. By liquidating the kulaks he eliminated the last holders of capital in Russia other than the state. The pattern of the Soviet economy was then fixed: all its human and physical resources would be directed to realizing the state plan, regardless of cost, human or economic.

The task of socialism was thus redefined as to enable backward nations to catch up with advanced nations by means of forced industrialization. This argument was to be immensely influential in the Third World after 1950, and, generalized into the proposition that an optimum allocation of resources must guarantee the full use of potential as well as actual resources, influenced growth policy in the First World in the 1960s too. The Stalinist command economy, instituted in the first five-year plan in 1929, came to be seen as a bold solution to the problem of extracting enough saving from the population to pay for rapid industrialization in the absence of foreign capital. 'Primitive socialist accumulation' would enable the Soviet Union first to catch up, then to overtake the West, thus proving the superiority of the socialist system and making possible the 'withering away' of the state. The key technical requirement was limiting the wages fund and the supply of consumer goods, thus freeing up investment resources for the construction of gigantic industrial complexes all over the Urals and Siberia. Thus was the revenue economy reborn in its modern totalitarian form.

The Stalinist dictatorship came to be seen as a disagreeable necessity on the road to bliss. This is to get the dynamics of the system the wrong way round. The Stalinist command economy was not a technical solution to the economic problem of inadequate saving and investment: it was a device for maximizing and perpetuating the power of the state. The command economy did not make totalitarian dictatorship necessary: totalitarian dictatorship made the command economy necessary. Only on this hypothesis can one explain the consistent failure to reform the system once its ideological and economic bankruptcy was apparent.

Dictatorship was justified by the need to defend the proletarian revolution from its class enemies, at home and abroad. From Stalin to Gorbachev the argument was presented in almost identical terms. In 1956 Khrushchev admitted that this justification for internal terror was bogus,[4] but the need to mobilize society against class enemies abroad was still proclaimed. George Orwell, in his novel *1984*, understood the need for the totalitarian state to maintain the illusion of perpetual war in order to legitimize its total control. Many Western intellectuals argued that it was capitalism which needed war production to keep it going, but, while there were powerful interests in Western nations whose upkeep depended on the war threat, the Soviet dictatorship was nothing more than the sum of such interests. For the Soviet state allowed neither a commercial nor a political market for the entry of any interests other than its own. The Soviet command economy was in fact what Marx imagined capitalism to be – an institutionalized system for centralizing wealth and power. 'Never, under any previous system,' writes Kornai, 'has so small a group of people kept so tight a hold on the nation-wide investment–consumption ratio.'[5] The gap which the Soviet economy developed between its productive power and its ability to satisfy human wants was exactly the one Marx predicted for capitalist economies.

The tight nexus which bound the command economy to growth and growth to military production was to prove fatal for the regime, for it produced waste on a scale unimaginable under capitalism. Hayek's comment in 1935 on the 'colossal instruments of production' being developed in Stalinist Russia remains pertinent to everything which happened later: 'The best tractor factory may not be an asset, and the capital invested in it is a sheer loss, if the labour which the tractor replaces is cheaper than the cost of the material and labour which goes to make a tractor, *plus* interest.'[6]

The economic imagination of the West has been profoundly influenced by the seeming success and eventual failure of the Soviet model. In the 1930s the gargantuan power of the Soviet industrial machine – all that smoke and pollution – provided an irresistible contrast to the idle factories and dole queues in the industrial West. In the Second World War it was the huge Soviet tanks which hurled back the invading Germans in the great tank battles of 1943 that impressed. In the 1950s it was the prodigious growth rates being chalked up by the Soviet economy, portrayed in official statistics, which persuaded many developing countries to follow the polluting route to modernization, and helped frighten industrial nations into 'planning for growth'. Conversely, the stagnation of the Soviet system after 1970 helped turn the non-Communist imagination against collectivism. Now the Soviet Union seemed less a prefiguration of future vitality than a foretaste of the diseases in store for a society which took the collectivist path. The revival of the free market in the West was built on the decrepitude of Soviet planning.

What was the record? It is now recognized that Soviet statistics 'exaggerated Soviet economic growth, efficiency and price stability'.[7] Not only were claimed growth rates consistently higher than real growth rates, but much less of the real output growth went towards raising living standards than in free economies. In the 1960s Brezhnev used to claim that Soviet industrial production was growing at 10 per cent a year compared to the United States' 3.4 per cent. In fact in the 1970s Soviet output growth was stagnant, and by the end of the 1970s it was being reversed. Over the whole Soviet era there was no catch-up with the West, and by the end of it the gap was widening. The Soviet Union's real GNP was never half that of the United States, as Samuelson believed in the 1960s,[8] but more like a third to a quarter as high, with a larger population. And, since a much smaller percentage of it was devoted to personal consumption, living standards were proportionally even lower. In the voucher auctions of the early 1990s, the whole of Soviet industry was valued at $5 billion – the price of one of the United States' larger companies. That valuation was much too low, but it shows the enormity of the gap between the two countries.

Even abstracting from the extent to which they were 'cooked' all the way down the productive chain, Soviet growth statistics were doubly flawed: they measured only the growth of physical output – tons of this, lengths of that, the so-called 'net material product' – and did so by assuming zero inflation. (The habit of demanding – and measuring – output in tons accounts for the *heaviness* of so many Soviet goods: Khrushchev used to complain that it was impossible to get Russian chandeliers to hang up without bringing down the ceiling!) A recalculation in terms of real national income in 1987 by the Soviet economists Grigori Khanin and V. Selyunin, taking hidden inflation into account, showed that over the whole planning period, 1928–87, real national income grew at 3.3 per cent a year, not the annual 7.9 per cent recorded by the official figures – that is, it expanded sevenfold, not the official 89.5 times. At an enormously higher cost, the Soviet Union managed to achieve the same growth rate as that of the United States. Khanin identifies an actual 20 per cent decline in real national income under the first five-year plan (1928–33), disguised by rampant hidden inflation. The decline over the five-year period was greater than that experienced by the West over the same period (which included the three-year drop in the Great Depression, 1929–32), and was associated with a 'demographic disaster' (i.e. famine and mass murder) which is estimated to have cost 30 million lives. In seizing the agricultural capital stock, Stalin managed to destroy much of it – so much so that wealth was being pumped from industry to agriculture in the early 1930s, directly opposite to what collectivization was meant to achieve. (Similarly Mao Tse-tung's 'Great Leap Forward' to agricultural collectivization between 1958 and 1961 proved to be a great leap backwards, national output falling by 15 per cent or more over the period.) It is ironic, but tragic, that many Western intellectuals embraced Communism in the 1930s on the basis of false statistics.

Khanin and Selyunin date the decline of the Soviet economy not from the 1970s but from the early 1960s. The Soviet economy remained viable due to the abundance of resources available to the regime. 'But the price was high . . . living standards fell for decades.' Over the planning period as a whole, outputs grew much more slowly than inputs, confirming that much investment was wasted. In the 1980s three times more inputs were required for a similar physical product than in the West – leaving aside differences in quality.[9]

What was worse was that output growth, such as it was, did comparatively little to raise the standard of living of the Russian people: goods designed solely at the whim of the planner 'destroy social wealth by using up material, capital and labour inputs, and hence should be accounted for as a natural disaster'.[10] Soviet achievements in space exploration and military matters were not reflected in the civilian sector. This was true of the COMECON system as a whole. Kornai shows that, starting from roughly the same point in 1945, the East German worker in 1970 had to work between three and ten times longer than his West German counterpart for most of the standard articles of consumption. (Some of the attempts to increase consumer satisfaction were comical. The People's Economy Plan for the Borough of Prenzlauer Berg (East Germany) decreed that book-holdings in the library were to be increased from 350,000 volumes to 450,000 volumes, and the number of borrowings was to go up by 108.2 per cent.)[11] The enforced saving of one generation produced no abundance for the next. Shortages of all consumer goods (except for party officials) became more pronounced as time went on: in the Soviet Union and Eastern Europe, much of every housewife's day was spent in queues.

Consumers also had to choose between goods of incredibly poor quality. According to the Soviet economist Abel Aganbegyan, 'more than two thousand times a year colour television sets catch fire in Moscow alone. Together with them the houses burn.'[12] Though the state provided the population with basic economic security, including guaranteed full employment, collectively provided goods were inferior in quality, partly because the share of GNP devoted to them was low: the health of the Soviet population actually started to decline in the 1970s. And, of course, 'lifelong solicitude is paired with lifelong surveillance'.[13] Measured by money income, the distribution of material welfare was more equal in Communist than in capitalist countries. But the difference was less clear-cut if perks to officials, administered benefits, black-market profits, and regional differences are included.[14] Social mobility was not markedly greater in Communist than in capitalist countries.

Why was the Soviet system such a failure in its own terms? The system's chief deficiency was the unprofitability of its investments. Although based on the principle of investing more of its national income than a capitalist society could achieve, the regime could not make enough from its investments to support itself. Eventually it drowned in a sea of debt.

There were two main reasons. The first was the irrationality of investment. The system of planning control relied on imperative targets and target enforcement through statistical reporting. This form of control is easily evaded. Throughout the Soviet era over-reporting of production and under-reporting of capacity was endemic. The use of non-price indicators deformed the whole character of production. The quantum which the indicator measured became the principal purpose of production. The only utility which plan-monitored production fulfilled was the fulfilment of the plan: a one-ton nail was as good as a million nails. Further, the combination of imperfect information, bad management and the systematic preferences of the planners produced serious structural imbalances in the pattern of investment spending across the economy. For example, there were notable shortfalls in funds for distribution, repair and project completion and, as in time they became cumulative, they depressed the marginal productivity of investment spending still further.

Secondly, the emphasis on quantitative growth discouraged the growth of factor productivity. The system could not innovate technically, and provided positive disincentives – from cost-plus pricing to profit confiscation – to achieving cost reductions. The slow growth of factor productivity was itself a constraint on growth. But, as the Soviet Union reached the point of maximum exploitation of its human and physical resources, it reached an absolute limit to growth. As this limit increasingly imposed itself, the capital cost of growth rose rapidly, and the return on investment fell correspondingly.

Improbably, the Soviet economy exhausted the bounty of Mother Russia. Disastrous returns to agriculture meant that population could no longer be transferred on a large scale from agricultural to industrial regions, and acute labour shortages developed in the industrialized north-west. Systematic underpricing of energy exhausted the near fields of Siberia. Rising costs, fixed prices and weakening labour control made industry more and more unprofitable, and thus undermined the revenue of the state.

After a visit to Russia in 1925, Keynes predicted that 'at a low level of efficiency the system does function and possesses elements of permanence'. The Soviet system went on functioning for sixty years or more. There were failed attempts to make it more dynamic by Khrushchev in the 1950s and by prime minister Kosygin in the 1960s. They sought to 'perfect' the planning system (Soviet code for 'improve its abysmal functioning') by streamlining the state bureaucracy, devolving responsibility to regions (Khrushchev) or enterprise managers (Kosygin), and increasing the supply of consumer goods. Khrushchev was the real instigator of *glasnost* (openness), arguing that 'inexhaustible' productive reserves could be tapped through 'the release of popular initiative'.[15] Kosygin stressed greater managerial autonomy over investment decisions. These initiatives all ended in the reimposition of central control. Like the West in the 1960s, the Soviet Union embarked on a fruitless quest for rationality through the computer.

Reform failed because 'democratic centralism' was the condition of the dictatorship of the Communist Party. The central planning system could not be dismantled, because it served the welfare of the party-state. No experiments in 'market socialism' were possible, except on peripheries like Hungary, because these would have endangered the position of the core. For the *nomenklatura*, general shortage was the condition of privileged consumption.

The decadent phase of Soviet planning started under Brezhnev in 1964. Brezhnev Communism was Stalinism minus the terror, and minus most of the ideology – totalitarianism gone flabby. It stood for rule by a privileged bureaucracy, a still militarized command economy, a media monopoly, police controls over everyone, and a confrontational attitude to the United States. As one defector put it in 1978, 'Just count up how many we have of ministers, deputy ministers, heads of chief administrations and trusts, directors, secretaries of regional and district party committees, academicians, writers, officers, and generals, etc., etc., down to policemen, heads of sectors, university departments, housing administrators . . . This system is their system.'[16] A Brezhnev mafia grew up living off privileged consumption rights and condoned black-market activities. Shortages and queues for practically everything became universal as wages outstripped consumer-goods production, leaving a 'monetary overhang' for bribery and the black economy. Transport, infrastructure, storage and distribution, and social services were neglected. Agriculture stagnated, despite spectacular land-reclamation projects.

The easing of terror meant that the central authority gradually lost control of the planning system to the enterprise directors and the Soviet republics. A neo-feudal society reestablished itself in the Central Asian republics and the Caucasus: 'Whole republics became criminal networks led by the first party secretary.'[17] This drained the state budget of revenues.

Apart from the priority given to military means, the plan had no political objectives. It became a monument to bureaucratic infighting, inertia, muddle, self-deception and venality.

From this time onwards, too, the virtue drained out of the Communist systems in Eastern Europe. The Communist élites were composed of time-servers and cynics. Gustáv Husák's new social contract in Czechoslovakia after the invasion of 1968 was: forget the past and your rights in return for food and a quiet life. It echoed János Kádár's cynical boast in Hungary: 'Those who are not against us, are with us.'

In the 1970s the Communist bloc, like the developing countries, tried to boost economic growth by large-scale imports of Western machinery, financed by petrodollars. 'Western imports became a substitute for economic reform ... The growth based on imported machinery proved unsustainable, while large debts remained.'[18] The debts could not be repaid, because, apart from energy and military equipment, Soviet goods were of too low quality to be exportable in hard-currency markets. The West started restructuring technology in the 1970s, but in the USSR it was stagnant. One indication was the slow rate of Soviet computerization: there were only 200,000 microcomputers in the Soviet Union by 1987, compared with 25 million in the United States.

The command economy could not make the transition to 'intensive' (technologically based) growth. It could not release the resources required for innovation. 'Even if the enterprise is inefficient,' declared Yegor Gaidar, later Yeltsin's acting prime minister:

even if its products are absolutely useless ... it does not mean it should be closed, or the resources redistributed; it is part of the state organization and must be protected, supplied. After the first stage of industrialization ... no industry in Russia had its resources distributed to other industries; production would not cease because there was no demand for the products, or because there was a more efficient way to produce them ... This type of economy could be dynamic and could have a high level of growth, but only until its resources were needed to create a new industry.[19]

As Tatyana Zaslavskaya tactlessly pointed out in 1983, the 're-lations of production' had become a brake on the further de-velopment of productive forces.[20]

Nor could the Brezhnevite leadership cut its losses in foreign policy. It might have renounced superpower status for the So-viet Union, but it would not concede victory to the United States in the Cold War. Instead it got embroiled in a military adventure in Afghanistan. The US defeat in Vietnam seemed to show that Communism was still advancing internationally. Besides, the Soviet state *was* by now its military-industrial com-plex. There was no political object in the system other than to feed this. To maintain it the rest of the Soviet economy had to be starved, but this threatened legitimacy from the other side – renunciation of any 'welfare' objective. The only way to square the circle was by 'accelerated' growth. The command economy – the people – had to be flogged even harder. But neo-Stalinist incentives no longer worked. Here we see in ex-treme form the pathologies which were also affecting the political economies of the First and Third Worlds by the 1970s. By this route, the Soviet state approached its own fiscal crisis and moment of choice.

At the start of the 1980s no one thought that the demise of the planned economy was imminent. As Gaidar said, it seemed very stable. The composition of investment was unchanged from plan to plan. The price structure was unchanged for dec-ades. As a result, the 'idiot' economy went on functioning in its own preset ways, oblivious to changing demands, enormous shortages coexisting with enormous surpluses. The only tell-tale sign was the growth in subsidies from the state budget and central bank to industry, approaching 8 per cent of GDP by 1985.

The scene was set for the Gorbachev reforms of the 1980s. When he took over from Andropov – the thinking policeman – and the decrepit Chernenko, in 1985, 'the country was suf-focating', as he recalled, 'in the bureaucratic command system.

Doomed to cater to ideology, and suffer and carry out the burdens of the arms race, it found itself at breaking point.'[21] Gorbachev's was the third attempt to de-Stalinize the economic system without breaking up the Soviet state. Both because of his commitment to revitalizing the socialist economy and because the costs of stagnation had gone up, he allowed the process of dismantling to go much further than his predecessors. By the time he tried to draw back, in 1990–91, it was already too late. The cycle of reform and reaction was broken: it was the Soviet state which broke up.

Gorbachev's *perestroika*, or restructuring, had three phases. In 1985–6 the emphasis was on 'accelerating' growth [*uskorenye*] through switching investment to machine tools and reaching a disarmament agreement with the United States. Only the second turned out to be successful. Gosplan warned, accurately, that the machines required to accelerate growth could not be produced in time. In 1986 a 15 per cent rise in investment in machine-building produced only a 3 per cent growth in the output of new machines, though the plan required 43 per cent in five years. In 1986–7 the share of new machinery in investment actually fell because of bottlenecks. Gorbachev was unlucky in that energy prices collapsed in 1986, undermining the import component of the plan. The main result of 'accelerated' growth was accelerated money creation.

Gorbachev also inherited Andropov's campaign to improve labour discipline. Substandard goods were to be eliminated by bonus reductions; efficiency was to be raised through an anti-alcohol campaign; 'unearned incomes' (from private activities) were to be confiscated; wages were to be kept down. When the quality inspectors declared most of the goods substandard, quality control was quickly dropped. The main effect of the anti-alcohol campaign was not to reduce drinking – illegal distilling quickly made up for what was withdrawn from the state shops – but to knock a further hole in the state's budget, which was partly derived from sales taxes. The brutally pursued campaign against 'illegal' earnings led to the collapse of small private markets, increasing shortages in state shops, and 'monetary overhang' – accumulated wages with nothing to spend them on. Wage reforms led to increasing wage inflation. All Gorbachev's measures failed. The fall in world oil prices, the loss of the vodka tax, and the increased spending on investment goods all widened the budget deficit and inflationary pressure.

The second phase, signalled by the Law on State Enterprises, in January 1988, was designed to increase the power of enterprise directors and employees. State enterprises were expected to draw up their own plans, become self-financing (cover their costs from sales), buy their inputs from competing suppliers, compete for state and other orders, retain part of their profits, elect their managers, and decide on the size of their wage funds. Conceptually this was a key breakthrough. Imperative state planning was to be confined to fulfilment of state orders: the rest of the economy, by implication, would be set free to respond to market demand. In practice, decontrolling production and incomes while retaining fixed prices proved disastrous. Instead of supply being set free to respond to market demand, it became profitable for managers and workers to steal raw materials, food supplies, and components from the state to sell illegally. With its designated supply flows interrupted, the giant state factory began to seize up. Industrial production started on its cumulative decline. Enterprises increasingly relied on subsidies and credits to pay their workers. But because workers had less and less to buy in state shops, their wages accumulated as money balances or spilled over into the black market. The legacy of Gorbachev's economic reforms was falling production, a growing state budget deficit, suppressed inflation, and a burgeoning, criminalised black economy.

Faced with growing hostility from party hardliners demanding a 'restoration of order', Gorbachev tried to create a new political base for himself and *perestroika* outside the Communist Party. In an attempt to rouse the bureaucracy from its torpor he had taken up Khrushchev's policy of *glasnost*. The result was an outpouring of dissent. 'Gorbachev was beginning to cut away the foundations of the very system of power which had made him supreme leader.'[22] Now, in 1989–90, he went into his third phase: the notion of a 'law-governed state'. He removed the Communist Party from its unquestioned leading role in politics and economics. This, together with the concomitant breakup of the Soviet Empire in Eastern Europe – Gorbachev could not risk reversing the disarmament process with the United States by intervening to prevent this – marked the decisive break with the old regime. The Congress of People's Deputies, chosen for the first time in semi-free elections, elected Gorbachev president of the Soviet Union in May 1989 and repealed Article 16 of the constitution, which gave the Communist Party a 'leading role'. In July 1990 the party and state organs were officially separated, reversing Stalin's fusion of them in the Politburo. Gorbachev now governed through a presidential council while remaining general secretary of the Communist Party. His failure to seek direct popular election as president was probably a fatal mistake. Other elements in the constitutional reform package provided for the free election of republican governments. Boris Yeltsin became president of the Russian Federation in 1990. The Soviet Union itself was now starting to split up, with civil wars starting in Azerbaijan and Georgia and the Baltic republics demanding full independence.

Everything was now conspiring against Gorbachev. His political reforms, superimposed on a serious economic crisis, now precipitated the economy into a free fall. Political freedom led to an explosion of social expectations. With elections going on everywhere in 1989–90, parties tried to outbid each other with extravagant promises of social spending and tax cuts. With weak executives in place, the inflationary forces became explosive. Wages went up by 13 per cent in 1989. Control of both resource flows and monetary flows was lost. The budget deficit in 1991 was 16 per cent of GNP and was being financed mainly through the banking system. With the market prices of many consumer goods five times higher than those in state stores, an administrative price rise of 30 per cent was decreed early in 1991. This led to a rise in the producer price index of 62.9 per cent in January, and a rise in consumer prices of 64 per cent in April. The Soviet government tried to counter this by confiscating high-denomination notes. This led to a panic flight from the rouble into dollars and physical commodities, increasing shortages. A barter economy was forming.

The failed coup of hardliners against Gorbachev in August 1991 destroyed what little control his government still had. The result was the complete destruction of everything that was left from the previous mechanisms of government control. Until August the regional party committees still managed to grab something from the enterprises; after August they lost all their taxing power. So did the Soviet ministries. Power to control the economy had disappeared. It could be reconstituted only at the republican level. The bread supply to the big cities started to dry up – the classic signal for revolution.

By 1990 the basic issue had become the survival of the Soviet state. Five Soviet republics – Estonia, Latvia, Lithuania, Georgia and Armenia – had seized independence; ten others had issued declarations of sovereignty. In retrospect, it seems that Gorbachev's last chance of working with Boris Yeltsin in a structure which preserved the Soviet Union was lost when he rejected the Shatalin plan of August 1990, jointly worked out by advisers to both men, which envisaged a weak federal structure and a 500–day transition to a market economy. Gorbachev rejected it because he was not willing 'to accept a diminution of his own powers, a far-reaching weakening of the union, and large-scale privatisation'.[23] By doing so, he sealed his own fate. Yeltsin's treaty with the Ukraine in December 1991, giving it independence, ended the Soviet Union, and Gorbachev, its president, had no option but to resign.

How can we sum up the Gorbachev era? Gorbachev rejected the Brezhnev formula of stagnation under dictatorship, but his political weakness, his intellectual muddle and his penchant for bureaucratic politics meant that he had nothing coherent to offer in its place. As a result of his de-planning policies, the central organs of the state lost out not to the market but to the enterprises and republics. By decentralizing management tasks from the government to the enterprises, Gorbachev found he had shifted political power to the republics.

What made the macroeconomic crisis of the 1980s fatal for the Soviet system was the breakdown in supply. An economy can function without money, but not without goods. The economy was supplied with goods through the vertical links between the central ministries and the enterprises. Once these links were broken, industry and agriculture could not work, and consumer goods could not be delivered to the shops.

The Soviet command economy was a system for directing resources to the production of those goods required by the state. It collapsed when the state lost command over the production and appropriation of these goods. The Soviet Union ceased to exist when the means to pay Gorbachev's salary disappeared.

CHAPTER SEVEN

THE NEW POLITICAL ECONOMY

The shift in political economy in the 1980s resulted from a fundamental rethinking of the role of state and markets. In essence the state's role was redefined as that of providing public goods – goods which the market cannot supply – rather than that of supplanting the market in pursuit of state objectives. Thus the new political economy is anti-collectivist in the sense that collectivism has been defined in chapter 2.

This does not mark a return to nineteenth-century *laissez-faire*, even as an ideal. Few people think that the state's role should be confined to providing 'law and order'. Everyone accepts that the state has to provide a wide array of public goods, including social services, and no one believes that most markets do, or can, work perfectly. In particular, there is much more recognition now than when Adam Smith wrote his *Wealth of Nations* in 1776 that public goods have a specific and crucial role to play in underpinning and legitimizing market transactions. Nevertheless, the recognition that there is a border between the state and the market, and that if the state crosses this border, wherever it is drawn, society as a whole suffers a loss of welfare, is the start of anti-collectivist wisdom.

The most urgent catalyst of change was high and rising rates of inflation. These ranged from a modest 10 per cent a year in the 1970s in the industrial countries to about 60 per cent a year in the 1980s in the developing countries. The latter figure hides several spectacular episodes of hyperinflation, notably in Argentina, Bolivia and Brazil. Inflation was the most obvious indicator of state failure. As Keynes wrote in 1923, 'A government can live for a long time . . . by printing paper money . . . It is the form of taxation which the public finds hardest to evade and even the weakest government can enforce, when it can enforce nothing else.'[1] The eventual policy response of industrial countries to high inflation and widening fiscal deficits was tough anti-inflationary policies. As a result, unemployment rose everywhere and (except in the United States) stayed high through the 1980s and up to today. The shrinkage of Western demand transferred the pressure to the debt-burdened developing countries, and in the end to the Communist world. The system of market economy was restored, but with costs which cast a shadow over its future. In particular, high continuing unemployment removed any immediate hope of reducing the state's social agenda, as well as greatly increasing the pressure for protection.

Macroeconomic stabilization as such did not amount to a new political economy. It was the connection made between high and rising inflation and high and rising taxes and spending which brought the state's role into question. In 1960 the governments of the main industrial countries spent, on average, 30 per cent of GDP. By 1985 this was 47 per cent. Inflation was the most visible sign that the state was *trying to do too much* – too much for its own health and, much more importantly, too much for the health (or well-being) of a free society. But there were other signs: the rise in the share of national income spent by the governments of industrial states coincided with a virtual halving of their growth rates. Cause or effect? By the 1970s many, perhaps most, economists were starting to argue that state activity was 'crowding out' more valuable, and certainly more valued, private-sector activities. Adam Smith's insight that a ruler's extravagance impoverishes his subjects had been anticipated by a fourteenth-century Arabic scholar: 'When the ruler's attacks on property are extensive and general, affecting all means of making a livelihood, the slackening of business activity too becomes general.'[2] For societies to recover efficiency, dynamism and freedom, the 'revenue economy' had to be curtailed. Thus the crucial context of macroeconomic stabilization, supply-side measures, privatization, deregulation, trade liberalization and the other reforms of the 1980s was the rediscovery of the value of economic and political freedom.

This was not an inevitable context. One response to government failure is to try harder next time. If some regulation is failing to achieve results, strengthen it. If economic planning isn't working out, extend the plan. If an economic forecast goes wrong, increase the number of equations. If an industry is 'failing the nation', nationalize it. If inflation is getting out of hand, add 'additional instruments' like wage and price controls to the government's armoury. It was the rejection of such collectivist remedies for failing states which marked out the new terrain of political economy.

The choice facing governments in the 1970s was analysed by academic Marxists with their usual acuteness. The Marxists had always believed that the Keynesian–welfare economy would collapse under its own contradictions. The full-employment guarantee had rendered workers too powerful for the health of capitalism. Profits were being squeezed between rising wages and intensified international competition. The state had to step up public spending to maintain growth rates: this was the explanation of the growth policies adopted in the 1960s. But the squeeze on profits continued. In this situation the only way governments could keep up employment was by keeping down workers' share of the national income through a combination of incomes policies and inflation. The central Marxist contention was that in the end the inflation tax became the only way open to capitalist governments to maintain full employment. By means of inflation, governments tried to keep down the incomes of workers and lenders, appropriating the extra resources to expand the 'social wage' (the welfare state) and subsidize employment in loss-making enterprises.[3] This could not continue. Finally governments were faced with a choice: to revise the social contract in favour of capitalism or to move to a planned economy and the elimination of the private sector. Most Marxists, harking back to the 1930s, assumed that the first would involve Fascism, leaving socialism as the only progressive alternative.

As we know, the first policy was adopted – in part at least – and the second consigned to history's scrap heap. In retrospect this seems inevitable, but it did not appear so at the time. While Marxist economic analysis is generally acute, it always presents the choice wrongly. The centrally planned, industrial-worker-dominated economic systems which the Left wanted to introduce into Western Europe are the oppressive, stagnant and retrogressive ones; whereas capitalist society contains within itself the creativity and entrepreneurial flair needed to adjust to new situations – *provided it is allowed to*. Faced with not dissimilar crises in the 1970s and 1980s, capitalism *invented* its own cure, whereas socialism succumbed. If the test of a social system is its ability to go on reproducing itself, capitalism won hands down.

One important source of invention was economics. In his presidential address to the American Economic Association on 29 December 1967, Milton Friedman declared that inflation was 'always and everywhere a monetary phenomenon'. It was caused by the money supply rising faster than the output of goods and services. Since the government controlled the money supply, the remedy lay in its hands: keeping the growth of the money stock in line with the trend growth in the output of goods and services. This was Friedman's famous 'money rule'. Friedman also believed that economies were more inherently cyclically stable than did Keynes, and that the effects of monetary and fiscal interventions were subject to 'long and variable lags'. These arguments reinforced the case against trying to manage the business cycle.

In the 1970s, academic economics, especially in the United States and Britain, was dominated by the debate between monetarists and Keynesians. It was essentially a technical debate within macroeconomic theory, not a debate about the imperfections or pathologies of state activity as such: the money rule would apply equally to a government that spent 90 per cent of the national income as to one that spent 10 per cent. Nevertheless, monetarism was loaded with anti-collectivist implications. First, and most importantly, it indicated that the inflation problem could be licked without resort to batteries of controls over prices, wages, profits, etc. with their accompanying bureaucracy. It just needed a few people in the central bank. Secondly, it suggested a political economy argument for cutting down on state spending. Keeping to a money rule would be easier the smaller the share of government in the economy, because the more of the national income governments spent, the more likely they were to run into tax resistance and thus resort to inflationary financing. Finally, in association with rational-expectations theory – another intellectual invention of the 1970s – monetarism suggested that a credible anti-inflation policy would not be too costly in terms of unemployment, since businessmen and workers would rapidly mark down their prices and wages in line with the expected reduction in prices. Without such an assurance it is doubtful whether even leaders as bold as Ronald Reagan and Margaret Thatcher would have been prepared to risk the monetarist route back to stable prices. In fact monetarism was technically and politically flawed. The Keynesians and Marxists were right: inflation was brought down at the cost of very heavy unemployment, which in Europe has lasted till this day. And monetarist policy did not necessarily bring about a shrinkage of the share of state spending in the national income. American experience in the 1980s showed that creditworthy governments (especially those dedicated to fighting Communism) have no difficulty in financing large and growing budget deficits without recourse to the printing-press. They spend more; others – in this case mainly the Japanese – spend less. The economy may suffer, but there is no inflation. Monetarism American style – loose fiscal policy offset by tight monetary policy – was to prove a profound, if totally unexpected, catalyst for change in the developing world.

Another economic invention of the 1970s was supply-side policy. Supply-side policy is about improving the economy's productive capacity so it can deliver the highest possible output for a given level of aggregate demand. Again there is nothing specifically anti-collectivist about it – any Soviet economist would have agreed with this laudable aim. Most supply-side economists did, as a matter of fact, believe that the best way to increase the economy's productive capacity is to improve market incentives; but this was balanced by a collectivist emphasis on the need for heavy investment in education and training. The central message of the supply-siders at the start of the 1980s was pretty ambiguous: it was that cutting tax rates, especially top marginal rates, would increase economic growth sufficiently to finance existing public-spending programmes. It was never clear how this kind of supply-side policy would reduce the agenda of the state. In the United States President Reagan was led to believe – by Arthur Laffer of the famous Laffer Curve among others – that he could finance his planned increases in defence spending by cutting taxes by 20 per cent! The result – as most Keynesians predicted – was a record budget deficit which continued throughout his years of office, and which Bush has handed over to Clinton.

Academic political science provided many illuminating analyses of state failure in the 1970s without offering any very clear answers about 'what to do' about it. One of the realizations of the 1970s was that unduly extended states are weak states: their reach exceeds their grasp. This was the genesis of the 'ungovernability' thesis, succinctly expressed by Anthony King: 'If Britain has become harder to govern, it is almost certainly partly because the number of dependency relationships in which the government is involved has increased substantially, and because the incidence of acts of non-compliance by other participants in these relationships has also increased substantially.'[4] This is the familiar problem of corporatism, discussed in chapter 2. In the 1970s most Western governments had tried to develop systems of cooperation with the main industrial 'social partners' (big business and trade unions) to restrain inflation and guide the economy towards agreed goals. But the outcome was unsatisfactory, and the remedy ambiguous. The state could either try to make corporatism more effective or retreat from it. Many academics in the 1970s thought that the first was desirable or inevitable. Charles Lindblom of Yale talked about a 'planner sovereignty market system' which would work through the state's power of procurement. Businessmen in defence industries would be paid subsidies to waive some of their property rights.[5] The British political sociologists J. E. Pahl and R. E. Winkler talked of the 'coming corporatism'. The state would use its power of purchase, subsidy and regulation to direct functional groups to the goals of order, unity, nationalism and success. Winkler rejected as contrary to 'any objective evidence' the possibility that the state would reduce its intervention 'and trust more in the market'.[6] This was written in 1977, two years before the advent of Mrs Thatcher's first government. What these analysts never made explicit was that, for their corporate system to work, state contracts would have to be large enough to exert a dominating influence on production; or that an economy of functional blocs in which the planner is sovereign is a good working definition of Fascism.

Inflation may be seen as characteristic of a weak or failing corporatism – a symptom of weak governments and overmighty subjects. In a brilliant essay written in 1977, Fred Hirsch called inflation 'a vent for distributional conflict, an escape hatch through which excess demands are automatically channelled'. He outlined two positions: that of the economic liberals, for whom this distributional struggle was essentially artificial, a state-created intrusion of privileged producer groups into the harmonious working of competitive markets, and that of the Marxist Left, for whom it was inherent in the capitalist accumulation process, with the inflationary outcome reflecting a particular balance of social forces. Here again the solutions pointed in opposite directions: back to the market or on to socialism – or on to the market and back to socialism as we might now say. Hirsch himself saw no politically feasible alternative to the existing situation, bad though it was.[7] The merit of his discussion, and of many others at the time, was to raise explicitly the question of the requirements of social cohesion, largely obscured in the heyday of technocratic Keynesianism. There was great interest in models of social cooperation which did seem to work – in Germany, Japan, Sweden – but these too were starting to break down, though less dramatically than in Britain.

For many analysts, political democracy lay at the heart of the inflationary disorder. Economic liberals saw inflation as arising from the competition by political entrepreneurs for the votes of an electorate who wanted more public spending but were unwilling to pay the necessary taxes. In 1980 Milton Friedman wrote, 'As it has become politically less attractive to vote higher taxes to pay for higher spending, legislators have resorted to financing spending through inflation, a hidden tax that can be imposed without having been voted.'[8] A profounder logic in this inflationary ratchet was discerned by the 'public-choice' economists James Buchanan and Gordon Tullock of the Virginia School, who saw the 'political market-place' as an arena in which utility-maximizing politicians competed for the votes of partly irrational electorates. Politicians sold promises on false prospectuses. Voters bought the promises because they lacked a personal budget constraint.[9] Using the same basic maximizing logic, economic theories of politics were developed to explain middle-class 'capture' of the welfare state, the 'capture' of governments by small pressure groups, the 'capture' of regulators by the regulated. The picture which emerges from these accounts is that of a continuous tug-of-war between a predatory state which seeks to maximize its revenue and voters and producer groups competing for income transfers to themselves, with the reconciliation being effected through the inflation tax.[10] Monetarist journalists like Peter Jay despaired of democracy; socialists talked of the need for an irreversible shift of power to the working class to make democracy work.

A much-discussed area of government failure was the unresponsiveness of monopoly or near-monopoly public services to the wishes of their consumers. Consumers of public services were unable to get them to produce the services they wanted – or, when the public services were on strike, as happened with increasing frequency, to get them to produce any services at all. A notable contribution to a large literature on 'accountability' was Albert Hirschman's *Exit, Voice and Loyalty*, published in 1970. In a competitive market system, Hirschman argued, customers can 'exit' a service they don't like – that is, switch to another supplier. The alternative to 'exit' is 'voice': 'The firm's customers . . . express their dissatisfaction directly to management or to some other authority to which management is subordinate or through general protest addressed to anyone who cares to listen.'[11] In a monopoly service, only 'voice' is possible: customers have 'nowhere else to go'. Hirschman then considered the case of a public service (like education) which is publicly provided and financed by taxes but where exit is possible on the margins (for those who can pay): he concluded that the ability of the articulate to exit the service will rob voice of its power without improving the service, since no revenue is directly lost. The conclusion – highly acceptable to collectivists – was that in these cases the articulate complainers should be made to 'stay put' by denying them the right of exit: a 'tight monopoly' was preferable to a 'loose' one.[12] There are ramifications to this argument which Hirschman did not consider, such as the possibility or even likelihood that if the articulate and capable are locked into systems of monopoly provision they will capture them for their own interests. The main point to be made is that this realization of state failure can again be made the basis of an argument for either the enlargement or the curtailment of choice.

A related discussion leading to a different conclusion was William Baumol's 1982 theory of 'contestability'. He argued that the dangers of private monopoly had been greatly exaggerated. The crucial efficiency condition was ease of entry into a market, not how many suppliers there were. Even a market with only one producer will behave like a competitive one if the costs of entry to potential entrants are fairly low, so the market can be easily 'contested'. This argument was to become the basis of changes in anti-trust laws in the United States and elsewhere.

Practically all the discussions of state failure in the 1970s took place in ignorance of the effect that the new microelectronic technology was already starting to have in transforming the economic environment. The discussions were static and on the whole backward-looking. Governments' task was seen as managing national economies, themselves divided into blocs of corporate and trade-union power. Large industrial firms 'set' prices, and trade unions 'set' wages. 'Solutions' to the problems of 'advanced' or 'monopoly' capitalism harked back to Fascism and Communism. Keynesianism was in retreat, monetarism gaining ground, but unemployment – traditionally defined in terms of full-time male jobs in industry – was still regarded as the greatest evil, and incompatible with democracy. The Great Depression of the 1930s and its consequences were extraordinarily fresh in the memory.

Ten years later no one was talking like that any more. One undeniably powerful way of understanding why is to say that collectivism stopped working because what was to be controlled had become invisible, disaggregated or beyond the reach of national governments. This thesis was strikingly proclaimed by David Howell in 1984:

Big solid sectors, classes and Blue Book categories, the chunky raw material of the centralists, the state socialists, as well as the Keynesian demand managers, are melting, mingling and dissolving. The 'soft' economy, in which more and more people are engaged in knowledge-based industries and services, and in which physical manufacturing employs fewer and is less concentrated, has started to assume new characteristics which baffle economic planners. We seem to have entered an era in which economic cycles move in smaller waves and in which a new climate of stability, without central intervention, may be attainable. In this sense, therefore, the anti-collectivists and the anti-statists have won hands down . . . The corporatists, who rested their thinking on big unionism, big government, big finance and big industry, are seeing their edifice collapse . . . The computer and micro-electronic communications disperse power and knowledge, and therefore traditional political formations, just as they disperse and alter industrial and commercial activity.[13]

What Howell was addressing was the collapse of what Marxists call 'Fordism' – a system of large-scale factory, conveyor-belt production geared to economies of scale, and based on steel and abundant supplies of cheap energy and, initially, cheap labour. When, in 1973, E. F. Schumacher published *Small Is Beautiful*, advocating an economic system based on a 'multiplicity of small-scale units', he conceived himself to be in revolt against the dominant steel-based technology of his day. He attacked industrial gargantuanism in the name of human and spiritual, as well as ecological, values. Although he made a telling attack on the inefficiency of large-scale undertakings, he had no inkling that the miniaturization and dispersal of productive units would be brought about by technology itself.

We have seen how the technological determinists of the 1950s and 1960s thought that technology was making Sverdlovsk and Detroit indistinguishable, and that this would bring about the convergence of the two social systems. They were right in one respect: Sverdlovsk and Detroit have both largely rusted away, and with them the relations of production which both created. The new technology has been pulverizing big business. *Fortune* Magazine's 500 biggest American firms have been shrinking or 'downsizing'. In 1993 IBM shed 85,000 jobs, AT&T 83,000, Sears 59,000. The slack was being taken up by small and medium-sized businesses. With the advent of distributed processing, faxes and microcomputers, business is being broken up and returned to human size. Economies of speed and flexibility – 'flexible working' – have replaced bureaucratic command systems. Financial and commodity markets have become a giant computer game; young unskilled males have become surplus to requirements – as workers and as husbands – the list of ramifications goes on. The essential point is that the new computer and information technology has 'decreased the importance of economies of scale, bringing the benefits of automation within reach of specialists as well as mass producers'.[14] Just as the old technology determined a hierarchic, statist, corporatist world, so the new technology ushers in a new wave of market liberalism with profoundly transforming social consequences. Crucially, by favouring small businesses, it has seriously undermined the corporatist wage-setting arrangements in

Continental Europe based on the assumption of centralized business and union bargainers. The OECD is now urging European governments to scrap 'legal or administrative provisions which extend collective bargaining agreements to sectors, enterprises or regions that are not parties to the original negotiations'.[15]

The historically minded will see in this process a repetition of the forces which broke up the great mercantilist empires of the eighteenth century, ushering in the free-trade age. With the reduction in transport costs, the great chartered companies could no longer keep out 'interlopers'. But the case for technological determinism is not established by this or by later episodes. Much of what has happened is explained by a Toynbeean 'challenge and response' mechanism. It was the rising cost of energy and labour in the 1970s that sealed the fate of energy- and labour-intensive production techniques in industry. The microchip was capitalism's secret weapon, its spontaneous response to soaring energy prices, labour militancy and collapsing profitability. An important consequence of cost-cutting through computerization has been the falling price of unskilled labour, which, when resisted, led to the emergence of heavy unemployment in the 1980s.

Successful leaders require great luck: their ideas have to coincide with the times, and they have no control over that. But that is all the luck they need. Once they sense the coincidence, they seize the opportunities which history presents, and thereby rewrite the future. This was the part played by Ronald Reagan and Margaret Thatcher in the 1980s. No one who rereads the academic analyses of government failure in the 1970s can fail to be struck by the fact that almost every piece ends with an implicit choice: market economy or collectivism. Most academics pass the buck. They make all the running but at the last lap hand the baton to the politician. Keynes had been an exception: he knew exactly what had to be done to preserve freedom in his day. So did Hayek in 1974:

What is likely to drive us further on the perilous road will be the panicky reactions of politicians every time a slowing down of inflation leads to a substantial rise in unemployment. They are likely to react to it by resuming inflation and will find that every time it needs a larger dose of inflation to restore employment until in the end this medicine will altogether fail to work. It is this process we must avoid at any price. It can be tolerated only by those who wish to destroy the market order and to replace it by a Communist or some other totalitarian system . . .

The first requirement, if we are to avoid this fate, is that we . . . make people at large understand that, after the mistakes we have made, it simply is no longer in our power to . . . maintain full employment and a tolerable productive organisation of the economy . . . This can be achieved only by that steady restructuring of the use of all resources in adaptation to changing real conditions which the debauching of the monetary medium prevents and only a properly functioning market can bring about.[16]*

Ronald Reagan and Margaret Thatcher provided the ideological drive and personal leadership which made anti-collectivism a cause. It is no coincidence that the cause should have origi-

---

* I disagree with John Gray, who argues that Hayek was wrong to say that 'economic planning and individual liberty were ultimately irreconcilable' since even 'very extensive State intervention in the economy has nowhere resulted in the extinction of basic personal and political liberties' (in Dieter Helm (ed.), *The Economic Borders of the State* (1990), p. 138). First of all, personal and political liberties were extinguished over a quarter of the world where central planning was dominant. Secondly, they have been severely curtailed for long periods in many countries in Latin America and sub-Saharan Africa run by dictators dedicated to economic planning. Thirdly, for Hayek economic liberty, including guarantee of private property rights and free movement of capital and labour, was a central part of his concept of liberty, and these have been extensively interfered with the world over in the service of state aims. Finally, and most important in the present context, Hayek was talking about the logics of two incompatible systems. He did not deny that they could coexist up to a point and for a time, but he argued that this coexistence was unstable, with pressure building up to go one way or the other through the accumulation of problems like rising inflation or structural imbalances or both. On this point he has been vindicated.

nated in the United States and Britain. It was not that collectivist tendencies were most pronounced in those two countries – this was far from so in the United States. It was that corporatist and collectivist arrangements ran up much more sharply against individualist, anti-bureaucratic traditions which had no exact counterpart elsewhere, and such arrangements therefore gave less sense of well-being. David Marquand makes this point for Britain in his book *The Unprincipled Society* (1988), in which he acknowledges, with regret, that Britain's 'governing philosophy' of individual liberty and parliamentary sovereignty could not support the kind of bureaucratic or neo-corporatist developmental strategies pursued with some success in Japan, France, West Germany, Austria and Sweden. Indeed, for most of Western Europe anti-collectivism has not been a dominant theme of the 1980s, with measures to restrain expenditure growth and trim welfare entitlements being seen essentially as technical solutions to problems of inflation or stagnation. The next few years will show whether the severe problems of structural adjustment now facing Western European societies can be adequately promoted by this kind of tinkering, or require the support of a broader philosophy of renewal.

Both Reagan and Thatcher were 'conviction politicians'. The point was well made by Anthony King in 1987: 'Try rerunning the history of the last eight years with, say, William Whitelaw, or Sir Geoffrey Howe, or Francis Pym, or Sir John Nott as Prime Minister.'[17] Try rerunning the 1980s in the United States with Bush, not Reagan. The free-market cause was stridently proclaimed by both leaders, but without the stridency there would only have been a faint echo round the world.

Reagan and Thatcher both underwent a passage from unease to conversion. Reagan – of Irish immigrant stock and small-town, middle-America background – was brought up to believe that individuals determine their own destiny, and that America offered unlimited opportunities to those who worked hard. It never occurred to him to regard his family (his father was a shoe salesman) as poor or disadvantaged. In the Depression he became a Roosevelt Democrat. He 'thought that government could solve all our postwar problems just as it had ended the Depression and won the war. I didn't trust big business. I thought government, not private companies, should own our big public utilities; if there wasn't enough housing . . . I thought government should build it; if we needed better medical care, the answer was socialized medicine.' Following his experience of Communist infiltration and trade-union power in Hollywood (he was president of the Screen Actors Guild), Reagan started to re-evaluate his early beliefs. He now came to think that 'With his alphabet soup of federal agencies, FDR in many ways set in motion the forces which later sought to . . . bring a form of veiled socialism to America.' Filming in Britain in the late 1940s he was depressed by how the 'womb-to-tomb utopian benevolence' of the welfare state 'sapped incentive to work from many people in a wonderful and dynamic society'. He wrote, 'I have never questioned the need to take care of people who, through no fault of their own, can't provide for themselves . . . But I am against open-ended welfare programs that invite generation after generation of potentially productive people to remain on the dole.' He called Johnson's 'War on Poverty' programmes in the 1960s, which quadrupled the number of people receiving welfare cheques, 'a tax-financed incentive for immorality that was destroying the family'.

The homespun message Reagan preached in his years as a 'Right-wing extremist' first got him elected governor of California in 1966 and finally propelled him to the White House in 1981. Campaigning for Barry Goldwater in 1964

I gave basically the same talk I'd been giving for years . . . I recounted the relentless expansion of the federal government, the proliferation of government bureaucrats who were taking control of American business, and criticized liberal Democrats for taking the country down the road to socialism. As usual, I included some examples of Americans whose business or personal lives had been tormented by bureaucrats and cited examples of government waste, including one federal job training program that was costing taxpayers about seventy percent more for each trainee than it would have cost to send them to Harvard.

I said America was at a crossroads: We had the choice of either continuing on this path or fighting to reclaim the liberties being taken from us.

And in a televised address a few days later.

Today, thirty-seven cents out of every dollar earned in this country is the tax collector's share, and yet our government continues to spend seventeen million dollars a day more than the government takes in . . .
   This is the issue of this election: whether we believe in our capacity for self-government or whether we abandon the American Revolution and confess that a little intellectual elite in a far-distant capital can plan our lives for us better than we can plan them ourselves . . . There is only an up or a down: up to . . . the ultimate in individual freedom consistent with law and order – or down to the ant heap of totalitarianism . . . those who would trade our freedom for security have embarked on this downward course.

Reagan's campaign theme when he ran for the Republican nomination in 1976 was that it was 'time to scale back the size of the federal government, reduce taxes and government intrusion in our lives, balance the budget, and return to the people the freedoms usurped from them by the bureaucrats'. He viewed Jimmy Carter's election promise to implement 'national economic planning' and a 'fairer distribution of wealth, income, and power' as a code for Soviet planning and confiscation.
   The message in his inaugural address was unchanged:

In the present crisis, government is not the solution to our problems; government is the problem. From time to time we've been tempted to believe that society has become too complex to be managed by self-rule, that government by an elite group is superior to government for, by, and of the people. Well, if no one among us is capable of governing himself, then who among us has the capacity to govern someone else? . . . it is my intention to curb the size and influence of the federal establishment and to demand recognition of the distinction between the powers granted to the federal government and those reserved to the states or to the people; all of us need to be reminded that the federal government did not create the states, the states created the federal government . . . It is time to awaken this sleeping giant, to get government back within its means, and to lighten our punitive tax burden . . . on these principles there will be no compromise.[18]

Reagan met Margaret Thatcher for the first time in 1975, soon after she had become leader of the Conservative Party, and immediately recognized a soul mate. She was a plausible fellow-ideologue. The daughter of a self-made grocer from Grantham, a small market town in middle England, she was brought up to be honest, frugal and practical: suitable qualities, writes her biographer, Hugo Young, 'for the management of economies, small and large'. In the 1960s as a rising Conservative politician she bowed to the spirit of the age, with only one or two rebellious remarks. She accepted Edward Heath's vision of a technocratic state managed in a businesslike way, and as a free-spending secretary of state for education in his Cabinet in the early 1970s she presided over an enormous expansion of comprehensive schools and observed his collectivist U-turns without protest, apparently absorbed in her own department's affairs. The conversion started only after the fall of Heath's government. It was inspired by one of his ministers, Keith Joseph, Margaret Thatcher's friend and mentor, who later declared he had discovered true Conservatism only in April 1974. For thirty years, he said in a speech in June 1974, 'the private sector of our economy has been forced to work with one hand tied behind its back by governments and unions . . . We are now more socialist in many ways than any other developed country outside the Communist bloc, in the size of the public sector, the range of controls, and the telescoping of net income.' The authentic voice of Thatcherism was being heard for the first time, though the lady herself only uttered in the new tongue after she became Conservative leader: 'Britain and socialism are not the same thing . . . Let me give you my vision: a man's right to work as he will, to spend what he earns, to own property, to have the state as servant not as master:

these are the British inheritance. They are the essence of a free country, and on that freedom all our other freedoms depend.' On a visit to the United States that year she described Britain as an 'eleventh-hour nation' dedicated to the 'relentless pursuit of equality'. Two years later, in Zurich, she felt that 'the tide is beginning to turn against collectivism, socialism, statism, *dirigisme*, whatever you call it'. The Thatcherite economic programme developed in the 1970s involved cutting taxes and public spending, removing state intervention in industry, deregulating the labour market, and legislating against union 'monopoly power'.[19]

Margaret Thatcher has described the development of her own thinking up to the moment when she became prime minister of Britain on 4 May 1979:

With Keith [Joseph] I had come to see ever more clearly that what appeared to be technical arguments about the relationship between the stock of money and the level of prices went right to the heart of the question of what the role of government in a free society should be. It was the job of government to establish a framework of stability – whether constitutional stability, the rule of law, or the economic stability provided by sound money – within which individual families and businesses were free to pursue their own ambitions. We had to get out of the business of telling people what their ambitions should be and how exactly to realize them . . . The conclusions I reached fitted precisely those which my own instincts and experience themselves suggested . . . I was again asking the Conservative Party to put its faith in freedom and free markets, limited government and a strong national defence . . . If we failed we would never be given another chance.[20]

Reagan and Thatcher both celebrated the virtues of the family business person who felt strangled by high taxes and red tape from above and by union power from below. This is what gave their message its resonance and relevance in a world in which technology was making small beautiful. Shirley Letwin has argued persuasively that Thatcherism's project was to create

an environment of lawful freedom in which the 'vigorous virtues' could flourish. The 'image [of the individual] which dom-
inates Thatcherite thinking is not that of invalids but of people
being energetic and self-sufficient'; Thatcher's concern was
with 'the unrealized potentialities of ordinary, robust British
citizens', with the problems encountered by the 'healthy and
vibrant, rather than the sick, the halt and the blind'. That is
why the political method of Thatcherism involved a rejection
of statism or collectivism, based on the concept of people need-
ing to be cared for. The kind of virtues which Thatcherism
wanted to encourage were promoted by the family, not by the
state: the traditional family is the means 'whereby the moral
qualities, and in particular the vigorous virtues, of one generation are instilled in the next'. A nation 'with individuals who
exhibit the vigorous virtues, and with families that transmit,
encourage and sustain such virtues from one generation to the
next' will be 'rich, powerful, culturally dynamic and universally
respected by other nations of the globe'. From the point of view
of the political philosopher, this, as Mrs Letwin herself recognized, was (is) a doctrine of revival rather than a complete social
philosophy, aimed at the hopes and frustrations of a specific,
though expanding, segment of society. But, despite its parochial
antecedents in a specifically British problem of decline, it was
a powerfully evocative image for other societies which felt the
need to escape from collectivism.[21]

The political economy of the 1980s was the creation of policy
as well as of ideals and the unguided forces of technology. Margaret Thatcher's distinctive contribution was her privatization
programme: she sold off most of Britain's state-owned industries, and opened up the public services to competition. By her
actions she proclaimed what everyone knew, but had been unwilling to admit: that the concept of state ownership of industry
was dead, and with it a central plank of socialism. Privatizations
followed all over the world: notably in New Zealand, and in
developing countries like Argentina, Brazil, Chile, Ghana,

South Korea, Malaysia, Mexico, Nigeria, Togo and Turkey. With privatization has come deregulation of the financial sector and the liberalization of prices and trade. New Zealand has gone further in reforming its industrial-relations laws than any other country, sweeping away its whole system of compulsory unionism, national wage rates for different occupations, and compulsory arbitration. Now it is presumed that employees and employers negotiate individual contracts.

The policies which had most effect on world conditions were, as always, those of the United States. It is fashionable to say that the Reagan Revolution never happened, and there is some truth in this, but it is not the whole truth. What Reagan achieved was deep cuts in income taxes. The top marginal tax rate was slashed from 70 per cent to 28 per cent; the standard rate was cut to 15 per cent; millions of taxpayers were taken out of income tax altogether. These measures were intended to improve not demand but incentives to save and invest; they were partly balanced by rises in corporate and capital-gains taxes. It is not completely clear whether Reagan thought that cutting taxes would automatically balance the budget. He was committed to a lower level of spending. In this he failed. He achieved deep cuts in 'discretionary spending' – energy subsidies, some transfer programmes, job-training schemes, federal grants to state governments – reducing it from 7.9 per cent of GDP in 1980 to 6.1 per cent by 1990 – a saving of $250 billion on trend. But spending on entitlements – social security, medicare and retirement pensions – went up from 3 per cent of GDP in 1980 to 7.6 per cent by 1990. This, together with the rise in military spending, meant that federal spending increased from 22.7 per cent of GDP in 1981 to 24.3 per cent in 1983. As the tax cuts also produced a much bigger than anticipated decline in revenue, Reagan, in 1983, was presiding over the biggest peacetime federal deficit in US history – 6.3 per cent of GDP. A combination of higher tax revenue and lower spending then gradually reduced the 'structural deficit' to 2.8 per cent of GDP by 1990 – not large by European standards, but large relative to America's exceptionally low private saving rate. In the USA, as in Britain and most other industrial countries, it was welfare entitlements which proved the decisive obstacle to the reduction of state activity. There is a case, however, for saying that Reagan's budget deficits did act as a break on public spending: 'If Bill Clinton had inherited a balanced budget, you can be certain that the US would today be embarked on a far more ambitious programme of public investment.'[22]

The Federal Reserve Board's refusal to monetize the deficit caused real yields on US Treasury bonds to rise from 2 per cent in 1980 to 8 per cent in 1984. The dollar appreciated in real terms by 35 per cent against other major currencies between 1981 and 1985. This caused a large current-account deficit, matched by an inflow of foreign savings which helped finance the federal deficit. No one expected this apparently perverse sequence of reactions, and at first it was little understood. US manufacturing exports were crippled, the mid-West becoming a rust belt; protectionism became rampant in Congress. America's famed labour flexibility came to the rescue, and total employment expanded between 1982 and 1990. But it is the international repercussions of the rise in US real interest rates which concerns us, for it was this which ignited the debt crisis which in turn triggered off 'shock therapy' in most of the developing world.

The Latin American development strategy had long comprised two connected elements: industrialization through import-substitution and inflationary finance. The first created a dual economy consisting of a sector of heavily subsidized public and private industries and services and a capital-starved market sector of small and medium-sized firms deprived of export markets through an overvalued exchange rate. Inflationary finance arose from the weakness of the state's revenue base, in particular its inability to impose the cost of industrialization on the propertied classes. Governments spread the cost of development to the whole society through the inflation tax – a form of finance which we first encountered in the 1914–18 war. Inflation was ratcheted up by populist dictatorships which bought off discontent with programmes of social spending, and by

trade union-led wage push in the public sector. Brief episodes
of 'stabilization' when hyperinflation threatened were invariably
succeeded by renewed inflationary booms, with a progressive
weakening of the state's ability to finance its spending – governments ended up borrowing the money they were printing at
ever higher interest rates. At least inflationary finance in Latin
America brought real, if lopsided growth, unlike in India whose
combination of central planning and fiscal austerity produced
the unique achievement of near zero growth in per-capita income between 1960 and 1988.

In the 1970s, the West slowed down somewhat after the first
oil-price shock, but most developing countries went on booming, preferring in most cases to borrow petrodollars from the
commercial banks at negative real interest rates to cover increased spending on oil. Hirschman comments, 'As in myths
that demonstrate the danger of wresting secrets from the gods,
the policymakers abused their newly discovered knowledge and
applied to excess the magic formulae which had paid such handsome early dividends.'[23] Commercial banks were happy to lend
to governments and state-owned enterprises, on the theory that
'sovereign states' could not go bankrupt. The loans were partly
used to finance public-investment programmes, current consumption of governments, or even real-estate purchases abroad
('capital flight'). Thus high developing-country growth rates in
the 1970s were achieved by the rapid accumulation of external
debt, which rose from $140 billion in 1974 to $560 billion in
1982 (more than double in real terms), by large fiscal deficits,
by rising rates of inflation, by overvalued currencies, and by
distorted incentives for industry and agriculture. In the face of
the second oil-price shock, which started in 1979, most industrial countries adopted strict anti-inflationary policies, inducing
the worst depression since the 1930s. The switch to anti-
inflationary policy raised interest rates sharply, especially in the
United States, where it coincided with fiscal expansion. Developing countries suddenly found themselves with a far heavier
debt-service burden. In 1979 they could service their loans at
negative real interest rates of 10 per cent; by 1982 they had to

pay positive real rates of 20 per cent. The Mexican debt crisis of 1982 caused commercial loans to dry up, partly because the US deficit was absorbing an ever larger share of the world's savings. The developing countries now found themselves paying back every year more than they were receiving. On top of this, the depression in industrial countries drastically reduced the prices of their primary product exports. Export growth virtually stopped in the 1980s, and per-capita growth fell to 1.2 per cent: in sub-Saharan Africa it went into reverse. The four East Asian 'tigers' – South Korea, Taiwan, Singapore and Hong Kong – were exceptional in being able to increase their real export earnings. Like Japan, but unlike most developing countries, they had always been committed to export-led growth. The key to their continuing success in the 1980s was, in the measured words of the World Bank's *World Development Report* of 1988, 'flexibility in supply response'.

Countries in trouble were forced to turn to the international agencies for debt relief and concessionary lending. Economists from the Brookings Institution, the OECD, the IMF and the World Bank started to descend in droves to sort out their affairs, as they were soon to do in Eastern Europe. Their watchwords were 'macroeconomic stabilization' and 'structural adjustment' – injunctions which, translated, mean roughly 'get rid of inflation and don't sacrifice your exports for the sake of building up loss-making heavy industries'. Money creation must be stopped, budget deficits cut, and the exchange rate fixed at a 'realistic' level; there should be improved public-sector management, better choice of investment projects, and a freeing-up of trade and prices. There was very little in these reform programmes which was new: they were the standard conditions for loans given or approved by the international agencies. The plight of the recipients, though, was now much greater, and distress had spread to many countries, so the impact of reforms on the world practice of political economy was bound to be much greater.

In July 1985 a thirty-five-year-old economist from Harvard, Jeffrey Sachs, went to Bolivia to act as a financial adviser to the main opposition party (ADN), which was expecting to take power after an election victory. He had been asked to prepare an economic programme to stop the 40,000 per cent per annum hyperinflation then raging in the country. In two weeks he and a local team drew up an emergency plan for rapid disinflation, based on analysis of the major hyperinflations of the 1920s.[24] Let Sachs take up the story:

During the two weeks, I attended a cocktail party at which a middle-aged man came up to me to ask about my ideas. I told him about the idea of a decisive 'fiscal shock' to end high inflation. He said that Bolivia needed *much* more than a stabilization program. It also needed an end of tariffs and licenses, an elimination of subsidies, and of price controls . . . and so on. In sum, it needed a decisive . . . reduction in the role of the state in the economy, which should come in a master-stroke just like stabilization.

Frankly, I thought at the moment that this man might be provoking me to 'expose' myself as a free-market extremist; or that perhaps he was merely pulling my leg; or that he was engaging in extremist cock-tail party banter. I really didn't guess that evening that the man, Gon-zalo Sanchez de Losada, would soon lead a true economic revolution in new democratic Bolivia, with consequences for many other coun-tries, and that he would soon become the most popular and influential man in the country, culminating in his election to the Presidency in 1993. Goni (as he is affectionately known . . .) really invented the concept of 'shock therapy' . . .

Goni's main intellectual antecedent, by his own description, was Ludwig Erhard. Moreover, . . . he . . . [was] acutely aware of, and frequently quoted, Machiavelli's advice to bring forward all of the difficult steps at the start, and let the 'good news' come out gradually over time . . . Moreover, he rightly predicted to me that the radical steps that Bolivia was taking would have to be undertaken in most of Latin America in the coming decade . . .

I learned that 'shock therapy' can work in a democracy, but that it takes active management and executive dynamism to make it work. Shock therapy is not an announcement, or even really a single 'mas-terstroke' (price and trade liberalization, subsidy cuts, and currency

stabilization can be achieved at the very start). It is also decisive ex-
ecutive-led action over a course of several years. Our work in Bolivia
in the first few years involved fundamental tax reform; the establishment of an emergency social safety net program (the Emergency Social Fund); the first-ever debt reduction program under IMF auspices
(after months of heated negotiations); central bank reform; closure of
Bolivia's loss-making tin mines; an overhaul of the tariff system; and
so forth.

Sanchez de Losada had realized what Margaret Thatcher also
saw: that inflation is a problem in political economy, not just
in economics. It is a symptom of state damage, a signal that the
relationship between the state and the economy needs to be
changed. In the mending of the state, the cunning of reason
was powerfully at work, for the 'accident' that the commercial
banks were awash with petrodollars in the 1970s meant that the
collectivized economies of both the Second and Third Worlds
could postpone their day of reckoning until the pro-market philosophy had established its intellectual dominance. Within a
few years the services of Sachs would be required in Poland and
Russia, and the new political economy would become truly
global.

CHAPTER EIGHT

SHOCK THERAPY

'Shock therapy' was first used on the hyperinflationary economies of Latin America in the 1980s. It was treatment for a crisis.
The hyperinflationary crisis is signalled by a universal 'flight
from the currency': no one wants to hold the state's money even
for a moment. At this point the tax on the population's real
balances becomes wholly ineffective. The economy reverts to
barter, or to the use of a strong foreign currency, like the dollar,
and the state cannot pay for its upkeep. The crisis provides the
occasion and opportunity for shock therapy.

Shock therapy is a three-part cure. First, prices are liberalized, the exchange rate is lowered, and the economy is opened
up to competition. Secondly, credits and subsidies to loss-
making industries are cancelled. This immediately cuts back the
rate of growth of the money supply, reduces the budget deficit,
and allows the imposition of fresh taxes based on money transactions. Finally, the main source of the excessive money-supply
growth – the bloated public sector – is shut down or sold off
for whatever price it will fetch. A country which accepts shock
therapy would be entitled to foreign help to meet the 'transi-
tional' costs of restructuring the economy, including the restructuring of its foreign debt. The crucial requirement for
success is also the most difficult: a strong and legitimate state.
The crisis needs to produce a new government, or a new regime, armed with the authority to tackle the problems which
caused it.

In broader historical perspective, shock therapy marks the
end of the 'age of collectivism'. As most economists and reforming politicians came to see it, overambitious growth
objectives, based on subsidizing fixed industrial investment, re-

gardless of quality or efficiency, had saddled both Western and developing countries with unbalanced macroeconomies (in which aggregate demand exceeded aggregate supply) rooted in structural imbalances requiring ever heavier state subsidies. These imbalances were carried to extremes in the wholly state-owned Communist economies, which is why they led to a crisis not in the system but of the system. But they were present in most economies by the end of the 1970s.

In some ways, Margaret Thatcher in Britain was the first of the modern shock therapists. It is true that Britain was nowhere near hyperinflation in 1979, but hyperinflation is only the very last stage of the inflationary crisis, the stage of actual monetary collapse. It comes up very quickly and is reversed almost as quickly – and easily. The difficult part of the operation is to lower the 'core' rate of inflation – the rate to which most of the activities of the economy are adjusted. This can go on rising slowly for many years. The 'shocks' required to get the annual inflation rate in Western economies down from 10–15 per cent to 0–5 per cent turned out to be not less appreciably severe in their effects than those required to reduce the inflation rate from 50 per cent to 10 per cent elsewhere. There was the same wrenching effect on established expectations. It is sometimes now forgotten that 'the decline in industrial output [in Britain] between June 1979 and December 1980 was the fastest [till then] in recorded history. Industrial production fell by 14 per cent while unemployment increased by two-thirds.'[1] Mrs Thatcher was also the pioneer of 'privatization'. Since then most governments the world over have been selling off their state-owned companies to private investors. The demonstration effect of Mrs Thatcher's successful privatizations cannot be overestimated: it killed off any lingering appeal of the state as owner of industry. Nevertheless, the general model for the transformation of Communist economies to capitalism came from the developing world. Stanley Fischer and Alan Gelb have observed that 'most of the individual requirements for the socialist economic reform have been faced before . . . in Latin American and African countries where the combination of a weak private sector, political monopoly, heavy policy-induced distortions and macroeconomic imbalance is not uncommon . . . the challenge [in Eastern Europe] is unique in its system-wide scope, in its political and historical context and in the speed of desired reform'.[2]

The economic crisis which accompanied the fall of Communism had three general features. First, production collapsed. 'The communist system did not merely end, it imploded,' writes Jeffrey Sachs. Once the command economy ceased to be commanded, industrial production went into a free fall as wages exploded and resources were hoarded or stolen all the way through the productive chain. The consequence of economic collapse was state bankruptcy. Government tax revenues fell, and foreign loans, used to plug the revenue gap, dried up. As a result, governments took to printing money. With the collapse of state finances, the industrial structure built on state orders (the military-industrial complex) became unviable. Millions of people throughout the Communist world found themselves in the wrong jobs. These were the legacies which the departing rulers left their successors.

The decay of the Central and Eastern European economies in the 1980s resulted not just from the inefficiency of their national planning systems, modelled on the Soviet Union's, but from the decay of the Soviet economy, to which they were tied through the regional planning system of CMEA (the Council for Mutual Economic Assistance). This interacted with the external debt crisis. Since the early 1970s the Soviet satellites had been allowed to borrow in the West. Poland and Hungary in particular had realized that they needed Western technology to raise their living standards. But the policy of borrowing from the West in order to finance the import of capital goods was inconsistent with the principle of autarkic development enshrined in the CMEA system, by which the USSR induced the Eastern Europeans to develop large industries to process Soviet raw materials and re-export them to the Soviet Union in semi-finished or finished form. It produced growing external debts and no hard-currency exports to meet them: it was estimated that a quarter of the satellites' manufacturing output had negative value at world prices. The rise in real interest rates in 1980 simply exposed the contradictions in this development strategy. That year Poland's debt-service ratio to hard-currency exports rose to 96 per cent; Hungary's to 47 per cent.

In the 1980s the logic drained out of the autarkic system. The satellites – Bulgaria, Czechoslovakia, East Germany, Hungary and Romania – needed to export to Western Europe. To do that they had to shift from a planned to a market economy. But the Communist party-states of Eastern Europe could not reform their systems. There were too many ideological hangups and bureaucratic barriers, and the regimes were too unpopular to contemplate the short-run costs of restructuring. Hungary was a partial exception. Its New Economic Mechanism, started in 1968, was the first attempt to steer a publicly owned, centrally planned economy towards market disciplines; but by the end of the 1980s little restructuring had been achieved. The incentives for the Soviet Union to continue the system were also declining. In the years of soaring energy and raw-material prices the Soviet Union lost out heavily from supplying its satellites at below world market prices: hidden subsidies are estimated at $102 billion between 1972 and 1981. The growing economic disutility of intra-bloc state trading was thus superimposed on the fading willingness and ability of the Soviets to maintain by force quisling governments which had almost no popular base.

These contradictions were most extreme in Poland, the least totalitarian of the satellite states. The peasantry had successfully resisted collectivization in the 1950s, and freedom for the Catholic Church coexisted with small-scale private enterprise. But the results were no different from those in the other Communist countries. In 1950 Poland and Spain had roughly the same per-capita income. But whereas Poland's per-capita income increased from $775 a year in 1955 to $1,860 a year in 1988, Spain's went up from $561 a year to $7,740 in the same period. In 1980 the extreme austerity forced by the external debt crisis led to the birth of the Solidarity trade union under

Lech Wałęsa and the latest in a series of uprisings which punctuated Communist rule. Only the installation of a military dictatorship under Wojciech Jaruzelski was able to avert the collapse of the regime in the early 1980s. A stabilization programme achieved temporary success, but was destroyed by a wage explosion between 1987 and 1989. This was unbacked by any productivity gains, the wage rises just creating enormous excess demand and intensification of shortages. As in the Soviet Union, ending the command system without marketizing it was fatally flawed. Solidarity was able to challenge the regime with a campaign of crippling strikes, and to force negotiations on political reform. A semi-free election on 4 June 1989 led to the installation of the first partly non-Communist government in Eastern Europe since the late 1940s, with Solidarity's Tadeusz Mazowiecki as prime minister and Leszek Balcerowicz as economics minister. 'Both Poland and the Soviet Union', writes Sachs, 'ended the communist reform period with hyperinflation, intense shortages in the state-run distribution system, a burgeoning black market, and sharply falling industrial production.'³ Because the ability of the Communist state to command the economy had disappeared long before a Solidarity-led government took power in 1989, Poland became the first candidate for shock therapy.

'Our proposal is an economy based on a market mechanism, with a structure of ownership like that of developed countries, open to the world, its rules clear.' So said Leszek Balcerowicz in 1989. The starting-point was practical rather than theoretical. With monthly inflation reaching 54 per cent in October 1989 (almost 700 per cent for the year), Poland was in the grip of hyperinflation. It could no longer service foreign debts totalling $40 billion. Queues and shortages were endemic. Solidarity had a powerful mandate to govern, but it did not control the government machine. The 'transition to capitalism' was simply an acknowledgment of the fact that the state no longer controlled the economy.

Poland's stabilization plan aimed at eliminating excess demand at a stroke. Liberalization of prices ('corrective inflation') was designed to cancel the zloty overhang, realign prices to reflect costs and relative scarcities, and allow the reduction of food and enterprise subsidies. Inflationary pressure was countered by a tight monetary and fiscal policy backed up by a tax on excessive wage increases (the 'popiwek'). Currency convertibility was established by a radical devaluation (the zloty–dollar rate went from 1,339 to the dollar in September 1989 to 9,500 in January 1990). The programme was backed by a $1 billion stabilization loan from the IMF. Jeffrey Sachs has described the logic of the 'familiar classical economic medicine' as follows:

The basic goal was to move from a situation of extreme shortages and hyperinflation to one of supply-and-demand balance and stable prices. For this Poland needed tight macroeconomic policies with the decontrol of prices. To have a working price system, Poland needed competition. To have competition, it needed free international trade to counteract the monopolistic industrial structure. To have free trade, it needed not only low tariffs but the convertibility of currency. To have convertibility of currency at a stable exchange rate, it needed monetary discipline and a realistic exchange rate.[4]

It was further accepted that real stabilization was impossible without eliminating the structural imbalances which were the underlying cause of the macroeconomic problem. The economy had to be reoriented away from heavy industry producing goods for the Soviet military-industrial complex towards light industry and service and retail firms supplying consumer demand, at home and abroad. Capitalism entered the picture not just, or mainly, as an ideological choice but because it was only under a system of private ownership that new enterprises could be started up, obsolete heavy-industry firms be closed down, and state safety nets be created for the unemployed. A mass privatization programme was unveiled in the spring of 1991.

Jeffrey Sachs has presented convincing evidence for the qualified success of Polish shock therapy. It allowed Poland to end hyperinflation, cut the budget deficit, eliminate shortages, create a convertible – and reasonably stable – currency, import at international prices, provide for buoyant private-sector development – over 700,000 small businesses were started between the end of 1989 and mid 1992 – and develop a thriving export trade to the West. Real wages dropped by one-third between 1990 and 1992, but not living standards, as there had been little enough for the pre-reform wages to buy. The main failure has been the slow pace of economic restructuring, connected with the failure to develop a successful strategy for privatizing heavy industry. The result has been a large fall in output and a rise in unemployment, currently 15 per cent. Nevertheless, Poland is now the fastest-growing country in Europe, with private-sector manufactures and services increasingly taking up the slack created by the decline of the old state enterprises.

Poland's shock therapy was the model for the subsequent Eastern European and Russian transition process. In its application, this varied in both substance and effect. In Hungary there was a more gradual approach to financial stabilization, and much greater access to foreign enterprise capital than in Poland. In Czechoslovakia, which had retained an unreformed Soviet-type planning system until the last, the 'big bang' was a minimal bang, largely because market disequilibrium and foreign debt were relatively low. The Czech Republic has moved rapidly to re-Westernize its politics and economics under the joint, surprisingly harmonious, leadership of the two Václavs, Havel and Klaus. In Bulgaria, the most backward of Eastern European economies, the stabilization policy had only the most fleeting success, and annual inflation was soon running at 400–500 per cent. However, very high inflation rates and falling output were common right across the transition economies. The severity of the slump, clearly apparent by 1991, surprised even the most determined therapists, and augured badly for the Russian transition, launched in January 1992.

When Boris Yeltsin became president of the Russian Federation in July 1991 he found himself a prisoner of a still Communist parliament, and inheritor of a collapsed economy and a collapsed state. In Gorbachev's last year output fell by 16 per cent and the distribution of food supplies had broken down. The only organ of the once vaunted Soviet planning system which still worked was the printing-press, which went on automatically pumping out money: official inflation was 93 per cent in 1991, but black market prices on basic consumer goods were often more than five times the official price. Gorbachev also left a fragmented state. The fifteen republics he had set up claimed the right to issue their own roubles, to collect taxes, and to own all the industrial property in their regions. When the Soviet Union collapsed in December 1991, Russia was on the verge of both hyperinflation and mass starvation.

Born in 1931, in Kazan in the Urals, Yeltsin was the same age as Gorbachev, like him coming from a peasant background, but, unlike him, from an anti-Communist family of kulaks, evicted from their land in the forced collectivization of the 1930s. His father was sent to a labour camp on a trumped-up charge six years after Boris was born. Yeltsin ascribes his hatred of Stalinism to that experience. If he harboured dreams of revenge, he kept them to himself: the system was all-powerful. As a young man he concentrated on his job as a builder and civil engineer, showing no interest in politics. He joined the Communist Party only after he was thirty, probably to advance his professional career. Somehow Yeltsin, like Gorbachev, evaded the law of the self-selection of the unfit which governed promotion in the *nomenklatura*. He rose rapidly through the regional bureaucracy to become party first secretary of Sverdlovsk in 1976, where his ability to get things done and freedom from corruption – rare enough qualities in the days of Brezhnevite decreptitude – attracted the notice of a fellow puritan, Yegor Ligachev, first party secretary in Tomsk, not far from Sverdlovsk, who later became Gorbachev's deputy.* Yeltsin came to Moscow as a Ligachev protégé. Gorbachev appointed

---

* Sverdlovsk is now restored to its pre-revolutionary name, Ekaterinburg, the place where the last Russian tsar, Nicholas II, and his family were murdered on 16 July 1918.

him party secretary in Moscow in 1985 and secured his election as a candidate member of the Politburo in 1986, during the disciplinary, anti-corruption phase of perestroika. 'He [Gorbachev] knew my character', Yeltsin wrote, 'and no doubt felt certain I would be able to clear away the old debris, to fight the mafia, and that I was tough enough to carry out a wholesale cleanup of the personnel.'[5] He struck Moscow's ruling élite as a crude provincial *apparatchik* – loud on bombast, short on political skills.

Gorbachev's natural disciplinarianism and the press freedom ensured by *glasnost* created the intellectual mood in which Yeltsin was able to climb to prominence. As Moscow party boss, Yeltsin gained a popular following with his attacks on party time-servers, his sweep-out of Brezhnevite cronies, his call for abolishing the privileges of the party élites – all reported in the liberated Moscow press. He toured the shops, standing in queues with the grumbling Muscovites. He had the management of a department store sacked for hoarding goods to sell on the black market; he had eight hundred shop managers arrested for corruption. But he failed to support Ligachev's anti-alcohol offensive, and alarm bells rang in the Kremlin when he started to hint openly that the party itself was the source of corruption. In a dramatic outburst at the party's central committee in October 1987, Yeltsin criticized the failings of perestroika, personally attacked Ligachev, and offered his resignation as Moscow party secretary and from the Politburo. The Gorbachev vilification machine went into 'spontaneous' action. Yeltsin was humiliated, his nerve broke, he mumbled incoherent apologies. Gorbachev refused to accept his resignation. A few days later Yeltsin suffered a heart attack. Gorbachev summoned him from the hospital to a meeting of the Moscow party's central committee to receive news of his dismissal: he was relegated to an administrative job. A few months later he was removed from the Politburo. Gorbachev had completely outfoxed the wounded lion. But the experience toughened Yeltsin's will, if not his body. His nerve would not crack again.

At what point Yeltsin decided that the party-state was beyond saving is difficult to say, but after 1988 he certainly started acting on that assumption. He took up the cause of Russian nationalism against Soviet imperialism. Russia, improbably, was cast as the victim, rather than the centre, of the 'evil empire' – a role which might more plausibly have been claimed by the ethnic non-Russian subjects of the Red tsars. But it made sense in a context where the empire, represented by Gorbachev, had become too feeble to govern but was still strong enough to stop reform. Russian nationalism had a concrete material underpinning: it was estimated that Russia paid over 100 billion roubles to the Soviet budget each year, but got only 30 billion roubles back.[6] Monetary sovereignty was thus the key to price stability and structural change. Russia had to get out of the empire before it was engulfed by its collapse.

Yeltsin is in many ways the exact opposite of Gorbachev. Artless, sometimes boorish, prickly, impulsive, he looks and sounds like a typical old Bolshevik, a relic from the Stakhanovite years of Soviet construction. The intellectuals much preferred Gorbachev. Not till they understood that Gorbachev was leading them into a morass did they turn reluctantly to a man who at least seemed to know his mind. Until the coup of August 1991, Western leaders, in whom Gorbymania still ran strong, snubbed Yeltsin. The only exception was the disgraced ex-President Nixon. Yeltsin admits that his nervous system was not suited to the 'diplomacy, compromises, the delicate and intricate bureaucratic game, the cunning "Oriental" type of rule of which Gorbachev was master'.[7] As president, he has treated his rebellious Duma (parliament) in the manner of an aloof tsar rather than a parliamentary manager. He is a hard drinker. Accidents have left him with a bad back, and his health has certainly deteriorated (despite his well-known love of volleyball and tennis). He suffers from bouts of depression so severe that he spends weeks staring at walls, and is indecisive until challenges crystallize. But he is a vigorous counter-puncher, and is at his best when things are at their worst. At this time of writing (July 1995) the main question mark concerns his health. But it is too early to write him off.

Postwar Soviet leaders have looked to the economists, concentrated in half a dozen research institutes, to 'perfect' their creaking system. Yegor Liberman was the architect of the Kosygin reforms of 1965; Gorbachev's favourite economists were Leonid Abalkin and Abel Aganbegyan. Yeltsin duly followed precedent. He appointed Grigori Yavlinsky, the original author of the 500 Day Plan, to his first republican government, together with Boris Fedorov, an economist at Gosbank. But it was the economist Yegor Gaidar whom he commissioned to implement shock therapy after the August 1991 coup. Yeltsin plucked him from the Institute of Economics, appointing him his economics minister in November 1991. He was acting prime minister from June to December 1992, and first deputy prime minister from September 1993 to January 1994. Gaidar's face is moon-shaped, his body a rectangle; he has few political skills. Yeltsin found him an 'inflexible prime minister . . . rather theoretical in nature',[8] but he was independent-minded and resolute, and, above all, promised solutions. 'The possibility of financial stabilization is determined only by the political will of the organs of power and the professionalism of those who execute it,' he had written a month before he joined the government.[9] Unlike most technocrats, Gaidar had a clear political vision, which coincided with Yeltsin's. Macroeconomic stabilization and structural reform were impossible unless Russia broke free from the Union – 'either we could continue to discuss interminably a joint economic programme or we could commence the transformation ourselves', he declared.[10] Since 1985 Gaidar had been in touch with Western economists like Jeffrey Sachs, who was soon brought in to advise on the reform programme.

Gaidar has said that for Russia shock therapy was not a choice, but a necessity. 'I am absolutely sure', he stated subsequently, 'that an attempt in the autumn of 1991 to introduce emergency laws and to make the regions obey orders from Moscow would have been the prologue to the . . . outbreak of civil war.'[11] Instead, he embarked on the transition to capitalism. This had three features: price liberalization, restoration of state finances, and privatization.

The priority was to get goods into the shops, and the only way to do that was by liberalizing prices. On 2 January 1992 price controls were lifted on 90 per cent of traded goods – one of the boldest actions ever taken by a government. This was the 'corrective inflation' designed to eliminate monetary overhang. Within a day food prices rose by 250 per cent. But the queues – bane of the Soviet system – vanished almost overnight. It took time for the supply response to come through, and in that first year the Russians suffered terribly, their living standards dropping by as much as 50 per cent. They kept going only by taking to their plots of land and growing their own food.

Gaidar made heroic efforts to balance the budget. He cut military orders by 70 per cent, and slashed agricultural subsidies, social expenditures and state salaries. He set a new value-added tax at 28 per cent. By April 1992 he was close to his target. Under the threat of bankruptcy, he hoped to force Russian industry to convert to supplying for the market. But the shock was too great. The reduction in government orders was not met by a corresponding reduction in unwanted output, so the improvement in the budgetary position had its counterpart in ballooning inter-enterprise debt. 'The first reaction of the enterprise director under price liberalization', Gaidar said, 'was to increase prices steeply, quite regardless of the demand position . . . The combination of . . . restrictive monetary policy and the strong cost-push inflation produced an enormous . . . crisis . . . involving the enterprise arrears.'[12] The 'idiot economy' went on producing output that could no longer be sold. This meant that enterprises, and their workers, could not be paid. As Russia was the main source of energy to the other republics, the problem of enterprise arrears was also reflected in balance-of-payments deficits of the republics with Russia. Political pressure from the enterprise lobby in parliament defeated Gaidar's attempts to staunch credit flows from the central bank. The Communists forced the appointment of their own man, Viktor Gerashchenko, as chairman of the central bank, responsible to parliament, and he immediately turned on the printing-presses. In 1992 credit issues by the central bank to the government, the enterprises and the ex-Soviet republics came to 40 per cent of GDP. Inflation rose to over 1,000 per cent a year. Intermittent attempts to rein in credit creation – at the end of 1992, and again early in 1993 – broke down against the refusal of parliament to sanction bankruptcies. Thus were the politics of gradualism superimposed on the economics of shock therapy.

As 1992 wore on, it was clear that shock therapy was itself in a state of shock. Inflation was out of control, output was falling, restructuring was minimal. The results Gaidar had promised Yeltsin were not materializing. The shock therapists defined the problem as political. The Supreme Soviet – 87 per cent of whose members had been elected as Communists – was filled with representatives of the industrial sector. The military-industrial complex objected to the reduction in state orders; the agricultural lobby to the cuts in subsidies; industry in general to higher taxes and restrictive monetary policy; the investment sector to cuts in public investment; workers because wages were late in being paid. 'So, we undermined all the political bases needed to support the policies we were trying to promote.'[13]

Gaidar stayed to get the biggest privatization programme in history under way. His main motive was strategic: to build a political base to sustain reform, and to 'cut the umbilical cord between political power and the economy'.[14] As long as capital was politically allocated, restructuring for market demand would be limited.

The method was dictated by the sheer scale of the operation: 250,000 state enterprises, no legal private entrepreneurs to buy them, no capital market. Yeltsin signed the required privatization decree in July 1992, while parliament was on holiday. The programme was supervised by Anatolii Chubais, a deputy prime minister and an economist from St Petersburg.

The privatization law provided a mechanism for all Russians

to become shareholders in the economy, by issuing them with vouchers which they could use to buy companies at whatever price they fetched at voucher auctions. But Gaidar had to make damaging concessions to the industrial lobby. The law allowed managers and workers in medium and large firms to buy majority shareholdings in their own enterprises. Life might not be so bad after all for party hacks transformed into owners of joint-stock enterprises, provided the credits from the central bank kept flowing. Gaidar wanted outside shareholder control with no subsidy: what the new owners received was subsidy without outside shareholder control.*

Maxim Boycko is head of the Russian privatization centre. He points out that for privatization to lead to restructuring there has to be competition. Facilitation of entry into the market and openness to imports has been critical for the reform strategy in Poland and Czechoslovakia. Russia inherited a highly concentrated and uncompetitive industry, in which many firms were unique producers of particular goods, bought their inputs from specifically designated suppliers, and sold their outputs to specifically designated customers. The transportation and storage system was geared to these input-output relations. Moscow bureaucrats have tried to resurrect the old ministries in the form of trade associations and financial-industrial groups to facilitate collusion and finance from central bank: that is, to move to corporatism rather than to a market economy. Their interest has been to consolidate firms, not break them up. Existing firms rarely fail to get protection. Politicians have restricted competition at the local level through licensing. Privatization of transport has been slow. The bankruptcy law provides for endless financial 'rehabilitation'. Companies rarely

---

* The state retained ownership of transport, space exploration, and the health and education services, together with an equity stake in large firms of 'strategic' importance. Most small shops and small enterprises were allocated to the local authorities for cash sale. For the rest, employees were offered either 25 per cent of the firm free, plus 10 per cent at below book value, or 51 per cent at a still very low price of 1.7 times book value. Seventy-five per cent chose the second variant, which gives managers and workers majority ownership.

repay debts. 'As long as debts and negative cash flows do not result in hardships for the management, but simply lead to help from the government, depoliticization will remain an elusive goal,' Boycko says.[15] Competition policy remains 'a gaping hole' in the reforms.

Another lacuna is corporate governance. Ideally, managers should have high ownership stakes but not be completely entrenched, so that outside investors can oust them if need be. As a result of privatization, managers and workers ended up owning about 70 per cent or more of each company, with managers obtaining far more than they got in closed subscriptions, by buying shares in voucher auctions and from workers. Managers have entrenched themselves through workers' support. Workers and management collude to maintain their existing position with subsidies from the central bank. In a typical large-firm privatization, only 14 per cent of shares are owned by outsiders.

Three types of core investors have been created: private voucher investment funds; wealthy individuals and private firms, who made their fortunes in the last few years in trade and commerce; and foreigners. But outside influence has been resisted, often successfully, by corporate managers, with the support of their workforces. A key question is whether attempts by outside shareholders to enforce restructuring will be resisted through the political process.

The final obstacle to restructuring is the continued political allocation of capital. Most capital of Russian enterprises still comes from the state, and includes subsidies from budgets and directed credits from the central bank. Subsidies in 1992 from the state budget – amounting to 20 per cent of GNP – included import subsidies, energy subsidies and subsidies for making interest payments on already subsidized credits. Directed credits from the central bank – adding up to an additional 20 per cent of GNP – went mainly to agriculture, energy and very large manufacturing firms. Firms got credits through the central bank at negative real interest rates. Little progress has been made in privatizing agriculture. Small firms, however, have been cut off from public subsidies and credits, and private capital markets do not meet their need. Some privatized firms have planned equity issues, but how much can they raise without promising dividends, restructuring or a governance role to investors? Without bankruptcy, debt contracts cannot work. In Boycko's view, capital allocation is the main roadblock to restructuring. The central bank's lending policies are 'highly politicized, whereas the rapid inflation undermines whatever private capital allocation might be emerging'.[16] Thus the essential step to rationalizing capital allocation is to end subsidies and stabilize the rouble. Stabilization and privatization are complementary. But privatization on its own does not lead to restructuring if the government continues to print money.

While privatization was going forward, opposition was building up. The Duma refused to ratify Gaidar as prime minister in December 1992, and Yeltsin appointed Viktor Chernomyrdin, a colourless bureaucrat, formerly head of the state gas industry. Parliamentary politics were crystallizing round a reformist bloc headed by Gaidar, a protectionist bloc in which the vice-president, Aleksandr Rutskoi, was prominent, and a populist bloc of Communists and nationalists. Parliament rejected Yeltsin's proposals to strengthen the presidency. It tried to impeach him. On 9 December 1992 Yeltsin wrote in his journal, 'I came back to the dacha from the Congress in a complete trance . . . I cannot stand public beatings when everyone gangs up on you and pounds you from every side.'[17] Nevertheless, evidence of the emergence of a social base for reform came with the referendum Yeltsin called in April 1993. He received 59 per cent endorsement as president; more significantly, 53 per cent supported the economic reforms. Unfortunately Yeltsin went into one of his depressions and failed to capitalize on his success.

It was the dangerous coalition forming between the parliamentary opposition and secessionist movements throughout Russia which forced Yeltsin to act. In practical terms, some regions started unilaterally to discontinue payments to the federal budget; others refused to dismantle the command-administrative economy, placed bans on exports, blocked the privatization programme. The secessionist movement was partly a result of struggles over the distribution of tax revenues, partly a reflection of the fact that the state had lost its grip. On 13 August 1993 Yeltsin in conference with the leaders of the Russian republics and regions suggested a federation council to include all their chief executives – this to be the upper house of a revised parliament with broad powers. The proposal was not well received either by the Supreme Soviet or by the leaders themselves.

'Am I a weak or strong person?' Yeltsin asked himself. 'In emergency situations, I'm strong. In ordinary situations, I'm sometimes too passive.'[18] In a televised broadcast on 21 September, Yeltsin announced the suspension of the Congress of People's Deputies and the Supreme Soviet, and elections for a new parliament on 11–12 December. When parliament refused to disperse after a fortnight's siege of its 'White House', and tried to seize the state television station, Yeltsin sent in the tanks.

The suppression of the parliamentary uprising of 3–4 October 1993 gave him the initiative. He abolished the local soviets (regional councils), and reinstated his constitutional plans for a stronger presidency and a bicameral legislature, consisting of an elected upper house, representative of the major cities and regions, and a lower house elected by a mixture of proportional representation and first past the post. Gaidar, who had returned to the government in September, gave renewed priority to the fight against inflation, and immediately ended the indexation of the minimum wage. The result was a sharp decline in real incomes for most workers. Fedorov ended subsidized credits, grain procurement subsidies, and bread price controls; the central bank was put under the government's credit commission, which set macroeconomic targets; free purchase and sale of land was allowed for the first time; the privatization programme was extended to strategic sectors hitherto untouched; and plans were made to set up a stock exchange within twelve months. This was the last wave of shock therapy.

The election results on 12–14 December 1993 were a serious setback for the president. His new constitution giving him sweeping powers to rule by decree was approved by a handsome majority, but, largely as the result of inept campaigning, the reformers were in a clear minority in the 450 seat Duma, even more so in the popular vote. Gaidar's Russian Choice got only 13.7 per cent of the vote. The real victors were the misnamed Liberal Democrats, led by Vladimir Zhirinovsky, with 24 per cent of the popular vote. Standing on a platform of law and order combined with imperialist bombast, Zhirinovsky emerged as the most dangerous populist figure in Yeltsin's Russia. He embodied Russia's hurt at the loss of empire and superpower status, and expressed the resentments of its people against collapsed living standards and gangster capitalism.

Gaidar's was the first attempt to stabilise the Russian macroeconomy. Two further attempts, in 1993 and 1994, centred on attempts to control Central Bank credits to loss-making enterprises. Both were defeated by large monetary emissions, chiefly to agriculture. By the end of 1994 the annualised inflation rate was running at 700 per cent a year, though average inflation in 1994 was down to 220 per cent from the 1,354 per cent recorded in 1992 and 896 per cent in 1993. With output in 1994 amounting to only 52 per cent of the 1989 level, Russia had experienced an extreme case of 'stagflation'.

Was 'shock therapy', then a mistake? It was probably wrong to start a radical stabilisation effort without first securing a constitutional and political base for it – a task postponed till the end of 1993. On the other hand, Jeffrey Sachs argues persuasively that an early IMF stabilisation loan could have reduced the 'deficit' in political support by enabling the non-monetary financing of the budget deficit. This would have removed the need to cut state orders so drastically right at the start.

The structuralists, notably Grigori Yavlinsky, head of the political bloc Yabloko, claim that the sequencing was all wrong. Before inflation could be reduced to a low level the economy had to be 'demonopolised'. Agriculture, in particular, had to be decollectivised. Political opposition was the inevitable reaction to over-tight financial policies impacting on an obsolete, but still monopolised structure of production. A perverse cycle established itself, starting with an austere financial programme each winter and low inflation in the spring, then credit emissions to support the gathering in of the harvest in the summer leading to high inflation in the autumn, followed by a new austerity programme. The problem with this analysis is that high inflation redistributes free resources to the very sectors in need of restructuring, and hence delays the recovery of output.

The 'Keynesian-Communists', whose most articulate spokesman is Sergei Glasyev, currently chairman of the State Duma's Economic Policy Committee, reject political/structural explanations of the Gaidar/Yavlinsky type. They see inflation as caused first and foremost by lack of state demand: too few goods, not too much money. It can be lowered only by increasing state investment and providing protection for domestic industry. Such a diagnosis of Russia's ills is clearly inapplicable to a situation in which millions of people are in the 'wrong' jobs.[19] Leaving aside technical flaws in the design of the three stabilisation attempts, the crucial missing element has been Western financial support – an omission for which the West may still pay dearly.

Since 1995, a fourth stabilisation attempt has been under way, technically more sophisticated than the previous three and this time supported by an IMF loan. Whether it can be made to stick depends on whether the Yeltsin-Chernomyrdin team can retain its political strength and nerve through the run-up to the parliamentary elections of December 1995 and the Presidential election of July 1996.

CHAPTER NINE

UNDERSTANDING POST-COMMUNISM

The first reaction to the fall of Communism was euphoric. But euphoria soon turned to pessimism as the Sovietologists arrived on the scene. Many of them regretted the end of the Cold War, because they had made a living out of it. Left-wing academics in particular regretted the collapse of Communism, because of the damage it inflicted on socialism. They did not want capitalism to succeed.

There were more substantial grounds for foreboding. The removal of the two historically artificial imperia – American in the West, Russian in the East – was bound to release a Pandora's box of ancient prejudices and new problems. Frightful though it was, Communism, it was said, had at least suppressed the 'tumult of ethnicity'.[1] The Cold War had also given 'the West' a sense of identity and purpose which would now fracture. In short, traditional patterns of history would reassert themselves.

The triumph of the West was not all that it seemed, either. The emergence of the 'global economy' – in which the fall of Communism was simply the most dramatic episode – has coincided with a shift of competitive dynamism from the Atlantic to the Pacific. Both the capitalist West and the post-Communist East face 'structural adjustment'. They are burdened with high unemployment. Thus globalism has gone together with strong tendencies towards stagnation and protectionism, particularly in Western Europe.

The pessimists made the familiar point that the Enlightenment project, whether in its Communist or capitalist forms, was a false Utopia, because racial, religious and national feeling are more powerful shapers of human affairs than individual interest or class consciousness. Marxism was defeated in the Soviet Union by ethnic conflict. Its defeat unleashed ethnicity on the world, by exposing the hollowness of the liberal promise. Paradoxically, the post-Communist world is being united by 'free enterprise' and torn apart by race and religion.

If we look just at Europe we see that the collapse of the 'iron curtain' has destroyed, or radically changed, all the assumptions by which we have lived since the end of the Second World War. Germany is now reunited, and Western Europe has acquired its own 'near abroad' in Central and Eastern Europe, which clamours for membership of the European Union and NATO. These events have fundamentally changed the dynamics of European integration, have posed new questions for Europe's relations with the United States, and have opened up a vast area of potential conflict with Russia. The political logic of the European Union is no longer to prevent Franco-German conflict but to pacify or stabilize Eastern Europe. But this putative political role not only heightens the tension between economic deepening and widening, it also reopens the historical question of who 'controls' the eastern lands. The Yugoslav imbroglio has vividly exposed the fault-lines in NATO. Is the United States expected to underwrite the peace and security of the least stable parts of Eastern Europe? Or is this to be the military task of the European Union? If so, what kind of Union? And how will this square with a role for Russia, newly restored to the disputatious European family?

This puts the onus of navigating the transition on politics. But in our part of the world, at least, there is a dearth of political ideas and big political leaders. Politicians lack what George Bush called 'the vision thing'. This stems from genuine uncertainty about what to do next. The Left-wing creeds – socialism, Keynesianism, welfarism – are discredited, but the Reagan-Thatcher revolution which dominated the 1980s seems to have run out of steam, or at least into a brick wall. Community, citizenship, civil society, 'socially responsible business' are the new buzz-words, but the ideas they seek to express are fuzzy, and no one knows how to translate worries about growing social pathologies in developed countries – the breakdown of the family, the growth of violent crime – into a new agenda for politics.

There are certainly plenty of problems. But as the basis for prophecy they reveal little more than the power of dramatic events to unlock the pessimistic imagination. Thus the pessimists already write off the European Union as an archaic Cold War structure, ignoring the fact that it is an extremely powerful political invention for transmuting national rivalries into peaceful competition. The pessimists also ignore the pacifying potential of economic freedom. For much of the nineteenth century nationalism and economic liberalism were allies in the struggle against dynastic power and feudal privileges. Whether today's new nationalisms turn into orgies of 'ethnic cleansing' or evolve into civil societies largely depends on the economic context. There is no *assurance* that the emerging global economy will calm inflamed political passions, or that it will stay global. But there is a long history of economic reasoning to suggest that it will benefit all its participants. This ray of hope should not be dismissed out of hand.

Apart from short-term/long-term issues, being an optimist or a pessimist turns out to be largely a matter of disciplinary background. Economists are a more cheerful breed than historians, political philosophers, sociologists – and priests. This is probably because they suffer from almost total historical amnesia – if indeed they ever learnt history in the first place. Not only do they believe that the market will sort things out, given a chance, but, like engineers, they are problem-solvers, coming to new situations equipped with portable science. Economics is almost the last bastion of the optimism of the Enlightenment.

By contrast, all the non-economic interpreters of post-Communism come to it either with sophisticated theories of social structure and change or with wide historical culture, or with both. Sociologists typically fear the disruptive impact of the market on civil society. They bring to the collapse of Communism a pessimism rooted in the current pathologies of 'marketized' capitalist societies.

Historians also tend to be pessimistic, for the only future they can imagine is the past. Soviet Communism, they say, was an updated version of the multinational dynastic state: its collapse opens up all the old cans of worms in the Balkans, in the Ukraine, and elsewhere. Old nations are emerging from the shadow of newer states. Yugoslavia broke up into four new states and four autonomous regions, and it may break up further. Can an independent Ukraine hold together the disparate regions left over from the Habsburgs, Romanovs and Ottomans? Is not a reunited Germany bound to try to redraw the map of 1914 or even 1941? How far will history unravel – back to 1939, 1914, 1789 or even earlier? 'With the end of the ideological division of Europe', writes one pessimist, 'the thousand-year-old divides between Catholics, Orthodox, and Muslims return to the fore.'[2]

The economists and non-economists have almost no point of contact. The economists are concerned with how to get as quickly as possible from a command to a market economy. The non-economists deal with vast sets of connected problems ranging from foreign policy, security and peacekeeping in a post-Cold War age to the new political and religious geography of Europe, the legitimacy of borders between and within states, and the impact of free markets on social systems.

One has to make a choice. The premiss of what follows is that *all* the problems thrown up by the collapse of Communism, the end of the Cold War and the de-collectivization of economies will be more tractable if they can be dealt with in a context of economic prosperity. But economic prosperity is not guaranteed by something called 'the market'. Successful market economies require to be underpinned by a wide range of public goods which, in the main, have to be provided by the state. This does not mean that there is a uniquely successful 'model', whether American, German or Japanese. All market economies are flavoured by the distinctive histories and cultures of the societies in which they arose. The problem is that the present phase of 're-marketizing' society – whether one looks at the post-Communist countries, China, Latin America, India or

Western Europe – has been accompanied, and partly caused, by extensive damage to states. They have lost the power to inflict great harm; but in many cases they have become too weak to fulfil their necessary functions. The over-intrusive state has been replaced by the shrinking state, as people have lost belief in the competence and probity of governments. The post-Communist challenge is to restore the authority of states without re-collectivizing societies. State repair is the main condition of market-based prosperity, on which, in turn, depends our ability to tame, if not solve, the 'post-Communist' problems of nations, races and borders.

Three notable efforts to understand the meaning of post-Communism are worth attention. The first is Francis Fukuyama's 'end of history' thesis, first proclaimed in 1989.[3] What Fukuyama meant by the 'end of history' was the end of ideological conflict. Hegel's motor of history has stopped. With the collapse of Communism there is no coherent ideological alternative to capitalism and liberal democracy. The serious questions Fukuyama raised were why capitalism outlasted Communism and why political autocracy has almost everywhere yielded to multi-party parliamentary democracies.

Briefly summarized, Fukuyama's answers to the two questions are: 'science and technology' and 'the struggle for self-respect and reciprocal recognition'. The capitalist market system, Fukuyama argues, is the only method of organizing the labours of mankind which is technologically progressive. This is almost certainly true as a long-run proposition, but two observations are in order. First, technological progress carries costs, and there will always be an issue about how much societies are willing to 'give up' for the sake of material benefits which technology brings. The environmental movement is the latest in the long line of quasi-religious challenges to technology or, more generally, to the vision of progress held out by scientific-technological rationalism. Secondly, in the short or even medium term, technology and the market economy are only contingently related. It is often claimed that 'Fordist' mass-production technology favoured collectivism. The new information technology may be transmitting the doctrine of the free market, the message that 'small is beautiful'. But we cannot predict what the next wave of inventions will bring, or the demands it will make on our political and economic arrangements.

Fukuyama's contention that history ends with 'liberal democracy' is less plausible. True enough, since the French Revolution there has been a trend in this direction, as measured by legally enforceable political and civil rights, representative government, multi-party elections, national sovereignty, and so on. At any rate, all alternative governmental systems – dynastic, Fascist, Communist – have collapsed; even dictators now insist they are temporary. However, these were all *Western* alternatives. There is no reason to believe that East Asian or Islamic societies will converge on Anglo-Saxon or European forms of 'liberal democracy', or that they necessarily share what Fukuyama calls the 'universal demand' for the 'reciprocal recognition' of a common humanity.

Even in the Western world the future of liberal democracy is not assured: it is highly dependent on a favourable economic context, which is not fully guaranteed by capitalism but has to be secured by policy. Twentieth-century experience shows that, although economic prosperity does not depend on liberal democracy, liberal democracy is jeopardized if economic prosperity is lacking. The 1930s in particular showed that economic failure provides a powerful context for anti-liberal movements.

This points to the fact that liberal democracy cannot be an ideological end-point. Its great strength is that it limits or tames political passions. But it does not dissolve them. Because politics depends on changing conditions, political knowledge is cyclical, unlike scientific knowledge. In political life we can easily unlearn what we have already learnt – indeed we have done so many times – because we are never sure of what we know. We can never be sure why any political or social project failed – whether the flaw lay in the project itself, or in the conditions or methods of its application. Since large-scale social experiments, however catastrophic, cannot be decisively refuted by events, there is no guarantee that they will not be tried again. Perhaps there is a learning curve in these matters, but it is very gradual, and liable to huge memory loss.

Fukuyama's claim that mankind has reached its ideological end-point is thus false on two counts: it is hopelessly Western-oriented (ideology itself is a Western concept) and, even for the West, it falls under Popper's general refutation of historicism: we cannot predict the invention of knowledge, and we cannot predict the conditions of change.

Some of these themes were taken up and debated by the Oxford philosopher John Gray and the Harvard economist Jeffrey Sachs at a symposium hosted by the Social Market Foundation in London on 30 June 1994. Gray is a pessimist, Sachs an optimist.

Gray drew from the collapse of Communism precisely the opposite conclusion to Fukuyama's. For him it was part of the more general collapse of Western values, freeing 'non-Western cultures from the perceived necessity to emulate Western models, liberal or Marxist'.[4] Western civilization is in decline, East Asian civilization on the rise. Gray's pessimism recalls the horrified European reaction to the Japanese defeat of Russia in the way of 1904–5. The difference is that then the Asians sought to imitate the success of the West; now they have emancipated themselves from its failure. Japanese and Chinese models of political economy, Gray implies, are better adapted to the new Darwinian struggle for survival in global markets than traditional Western ones.

Contrary to Fukuyama, Gray believes that 'free-market fundamentalism' and 'liberal democracy' are in contradiction. The condition of liberal democracy is substantial social control over market forces:

The fact that the subversive dynamism of market institutions, particularly when these are globalised, destroys personal and communal security . . . is of central importance not only in the Western liberal democracies . . . but also for the post-communist states. For, in the latter, the collapse of the bankrupt institutions of central planning, and the subsequent ill-conceived adoption of Neo-Liberal policies of shock-therapy, has replicated in grotesquely exaggerated form the Western problem of market-driven structural adjustments occurring in conditions of zero or even negative growth. Entirely predictably . . . the political beneficiaries of mass economic insecurity pervasive in such conditions have, virtually everywhere, been neo-communist and neo-fascist parties, sometimes in combination. . . The fundamental truth that rapid and continuous market-driven economic change is inimical to settled community, and in the long run to the stability of liberal and democratic institutions, has apparently yet to be grasped by most Western policy-makers.[5]

It is not clear what is the crucial assumption being made here. Is it the undermining effect of the institutionally naked market system *per se*, or the fact that 'market-driven changes' have taken place in conditions of 'zero or even negative growth'? One of the recurring themes in the pessimistic literature is that the era of economic growth is over.[6] But there is no more warrant for this than for Fukuyama's contrary belief that growth is assured till all wants are satisfied. This particular source of pessimism seems to stem from the coincidence that the fall of Communism took place just when a cyclical downturn started in the West. But Western recovery started in 1992, and recently a number of post-Communist countries have experienced positive growth rates. Structural adjustment, and much else, is easier when the world economy is booming, not slumping.

It is from this perspective that Gray attacks the 'shock therapy' associated with Jeffrey Sachs. This ignored the *social damage* suffered by the Communist economies, the *failure* of market solutions to social and economic problems in the West, and the *dissolution* of the Cold War habitat of international relations. Former Communist countries – victims of decades of desolation – were being invited to join a Western capitalist community which was itself sick.

Gray's four main theses can be summarized as follows. First

is his 'conception of market institutions . . . as human practices . . . deeply embedded in matrices of cultural tradition and in legal and political frameworks, to which they owe all their stability and legitimacy'. This means that there is no single exportable model of market institutions suitable for all post-Communist countries.

Secondly, there has been a general 'meltdown of the various Western models of market institutions . . . indeed, in one of history's choicest – and cruellest – ironies, a legitimation crisis for Western market institutions, for which neo-Marxist theorists . . . had looked in vain during the decades of economic prosperity and Cold War, now seems to be underway, in the new historical context in which Soviet (but not, perhaps, Russian) enmity has vanished'. The historical record does not bear this out. The 'legitimation crisis' of non-Communist systems actually occurred in the 1970s and early 1980s and led to the Reagan-Thatcher revolution. These were worldwide crises of semi-socialized economies, for which marketization was the remedy. This solution was subsequently adopted for the far more severe crises of the fully socialized (or Communist) economies. Marketization in turn is beset with problems, but one needs to have a clear view of the whole sequence to understand what has been happening.

Gray's third argument against policies of 'shock therapy' is that they ignore the 'inherited deformation of the institutional and natural environments' of the former Communist countries. This means that policies for the transition to the market system derived from the experience of less damaged semi-socialized systems like those of Latin America in the 1980s are 'dangerously inappropriate'. The success of the post-Communist governments depends on their ability to protect their citizens from civil strife and organized crime. Yet the application of shock therapy to post-Communist societies has produced a slump in production, gangster capitalism and 'nomenklaturist expropriation and rent-seeking', all of them bound to destroy the political legitimacy of reformist governments. The results are to be seen in the defeat of the Russian reformers in the election of December 1993, and the return to power of the neo-Communist Left all over the former Soviet Empire.

Four 'programmatic' conclusions follow from this analysis: there can be 'no highly specific policy prescriptions that apply to all the post-communist states'; a gradualist strategy for transformation, tailored to specific historical situations, will achieve superior results to universal shock therapy; the provision of social safety nets is 'a necessary condition of the political viability of market reform'; and authoritarianism in Russia may be necessary to overcome the 'Hobbesian' problem created by the fragmentation of the Soviet Union. Only by abandoning a 'crude and monistic conception of market institutions in which they are misconceived as self-contained and free-standing systems' can Western policy-makers and advisers contribute constructively to the transition.[7]

Jeffrey Sachs comes to the same set of issues as a problem-solver, not a social theorist.[8] He is concerned not with the varieties of capitalist models – these choices will evolve over time – but with the need of the transition economies to establish 'core institutions' to make any version of capitalism work: stable, convertible national currencies; freedom of international trade and foreign investment; private property rights; private ownership; corporate control of large enterprises; and a social safety net. This basic infrastructure, he claims, has been successfully exported all over the world. The irony is that, for all Gray's emphasis on particularism, transplantation has worked very well – starting with the Meiji restoration in Japan in 1868. Sachs argues strongly for formalism – instituting the core legal system, and then allowing it to adapt to local practices. What Gray calls 'historical particularism' Sachs sees as extravagant fears always attached to fundamental change, however promising. The pessimists, he says, are always predicting that shock therapy will not work in a given country because of that country's particular history, and then using that self-same history to explain why it worked there but will not work elsewhere.

Sachs doubts Gray's assertion that the West has had its day

as the creator of values. He points out that the IMF and the World Bank were pivotal in squeezing Communism and collectivism out of the world economy in the 1980s. How central they will be to the economic order of the 1990s is questionable.

Sachs directly confronts Gray's assertion that shock therapy (a term he dislikes) was an *ideological* project. Over much of the post-Communist world 'shocking' was the only way in which collapsed economies, characterized by hyperinflation and rapidly falling production, could be brought back to life: 'the post-Communist leaders inherited complex, urban, industrialized societies that had already stopped working'. The nature of the crisis dictated the priorities: price liberalization, financial consolidation, privatization. Sachs denies any naïve faith in the automatic success of these policies: success requires 'vigorous political leadership'; also, international aid 'is critical to helping the reforms themselves take hold'. Sachs passionately believes that the failure of the IMF to provide support at critical moments doomed Gaidar's early attempts to stabilize the Russian macroeconomy; the IMF counters that the reformers never had the power to carry out their plans. Sachs appears to overlook the complexity of the infrastructural requirements of political legitimacy: vigorous leadership cannot be asserted in a political vacuum. That is why Polish shock therapy, based on the Solidarity movement, always had a better chance of working than Russian shock therapy, based on a very weak state.

The issue is thus more complex than Sachs allows. A decision to sustain Boris Yeltsin *come what may* could only have been taken at the highest political level. But the collapse of Russian Communism in 1991 found President Bush and other Western leaders otherwise engaged. Bush's attention was focused on the Middle East, later on trying to get re-elected; European leaders were embroiled in the Maastricht Treaty; Germany's hands were full with integrating its eastern Länder; Japan would not help Russia unless it returned the Lesser Kurile Islands, seized in 1945. Thus the period 1990–93 was a 'grand missed opportunity'.[9]

Finally, Sachs accuses Gray of confusing cause and effect.

Shock therapy did not produce the post-Communist slump: it enabled countries to recover from slumps which resulted from the breakdown of militarized economies. The more decisively it was applied, the faster was the recovery. *Nomenklatura* expropriation of state assets was the inevitable result of the collapse of the authority of the Communist Party. 'Mass privatization is the best hope to arrest this spontaneous process, by establishing a transparent, rule-bound system to divide the assets among the various stakeholders.' Finally, shock therapy has not so far discredited the reformers. Where vigorously pursued, it has established a 'national consensus on the broad terms of economic management', so that successor governments elected in Poland and Slovenia in 1994 followed the reform policies of their predecessors. The electoral support for neo-Communist parties is largely provided by pensioners and older workers in state factories protesting against income losses. Politics, in other words, is reverting to the pattern, familiar in the West, of 'a bidding war over social entitlements, in societies where the budget is already stretched to the limit . . . The danger in Eastern Europe does not seem to be a return to Communist ideology or practice, but rather the undermining of a fragile and hard-won fiscal balance achieved in the early years of reform.'

At one level, the Gray–Sachs debate is about priorities: gradualism versus shock therapy. This involves technical judgements about the speed, direction and sequence of reaction to 'shocks', as well as judgements about the political sustainability of reform. There is no right answer, irrespective of circumstances. The closer a society is to collapse, the less relevant such calculations become in any case. Spontaneous forces erupt, and the least bad policy for a weak government is to legitimize or decriminalize what cannot be stopped, and hope to regain control of events later on. A great deal of the transformation of post-Communist Europe has to be seen in this light, rather than as the deliberate application of a 'gradualist' or 'cold-turkey' strategy directed to an agreed end. What is beyond doubt is that gradualism within Communism (China temporarily excepted) failed. A political revolution was needed to unlock the forces of change.

At a deeper level, though, the Gray–Sachs debate is about political economy. Gray believes that market forces are destructive of social and political authority (and ultimately of the market system itself) and therefore need to be heavily circumscribed by, or rooted in, the non-market traditions of particular societies. A rich vein of sociological writing and conservative thought supports this view. Sachs sees the capitalist market economy as a portable package of practices and technical institutions which maximizes the welfare of the countries which adopt it and which therefore tends to strengthen their social and political systems. Democracy requires a market economy as the engine of economic success. This is the main argument for introducing one as quickly as possible.

The replacement of Communism by capitalism is an entirely novel experience in human history. No society has ever been centrally planned down to the last detail before. So the dynamics of the transformation are unpredictable. Conservative philosophies of change can offer no guide to the future. The social institutions needed to contain the new forces will have to be recreated from the fragments of broken systems.

The crux of the matter is whether Sachs's 'portable' capitalism can take root quickly enough to start delivering results. On this will depend, in part, whether the former Communist world turns out to be peaceful or warlike, liberal or despotic. Supporting a benign outcome are the lack of coherent ideological challenge and the integrating pressures of 'globalism'. Against it are the political and social strains of structural adjustment, which could still upset market reform and internationalism – and not just in post-Communist societies.

CHAPTER TEN

TRANSFORMATION TO WHAT?

How much progress has been made in transforming collapsed Communist economies into functioning capitalist ones? Have the reforms strengthened or weakened political democracy?

The Czech prime minister Václav Klaus suggested as a test of progress for transition economies the enactment of 'a critical mass of reforms needed to change the basic system and so deliver some tangible results'.[1] In a report published in October 1994 (updated April 1995), the European Bank for Reconstruction and Development has presented indicators of progress in changing the basic system and delivering tangible results for all twenty-five post-Communist countries.[2]

The main indicators of 'change in the basic system' are: (a) the share of output produced by the private sector; (b) the amount of enterprise restructuring, including improvements in corporate governance, breakup of monopolies, and bankruptcies; (c) the degree of price liberalization and competition; (d) openness to world trade; and (e) the creation of an efficient banking system. The EBRD report rates achievement in all these areas from 1 to 4, 1 showing little progress and 4 showing great progress. The typical developed Western country would rate 4 on all indicators. The report emphasizes that what is being assessed is the status, not the pace, of change.

Column 1 (privatization) in Table 1 shows that in Eastern European countries (those outside the Commonwealth of Independent States (CIS) but including the Baltic republics) the share of the private sector in GDP is now typically 50 per cent and over, with the Czech Republic (65 per cent) and Hungary and Poland (55 per cent) at the top, and Romania (35 per cent) at the bottom. (Poland started from a much higher base, since

TABLE I: PROGRESS IN TRANSITION IN EASTERN EUROPE AND THE FORMER SOVIET UNION

		ENTERPRISES			MARKETS AND TRADE		FINANCIAL INSTITUTIONS
	Private-sector share of GDP mid-94 in % (rough EBRD estimate)	Large-scale privatization	Small-scale privatization	Enterprise restructuring	Price liberalization and competition	Trade and foreign exchange system	Banking reform
Albania	50	1	3	2	3	4	2
Armenia	40	1	3	1	3	2	1
Azerbaijan	20	1	1	1	3	1	1
Belarus	15	2	2	2	2	1	1
Bulgaria	40	2	2	2	3	4	2
Croatia	40	3	4	2	3	4	3
Czech Republic	65	4	4	3	3	4	3
Estonia	55	3	4	3	3	4	3
FYR Macedonia	35	2	4	2	3	4	2
Georgia	20	1	2	1	2	1	1
Hungary	55	3	4	3	3	4	3
Kazakhstan	20	2	2	1	2	2	1
Kyrgyzstan	30	3	4	2	3	3	2
Latvia	55	2	3	2	3	4	3
Lithuania	50	3	4	2	3	4	2
Moldova	20	2	2	2	3	2	2
Poland	55	3	4	3	3	4	3
Romania	35	2	3	2	3	4	2
Russian Federation	50	3	3	2	3	3	2
Slovak Republic	55	3	4	3	3	4	3
Slovenia	30	2	4	3	3	4	3
Tajikistan	15	2	2	1	3	1	1
Turkmenistan	15	1	1	1	2	1	1
Ukraine	30	1	2	1	2	1	1
Uzbekistan	20	2	3	1	3	2	1

Source: EBRD, *Transition Report*, p. 7

most agriculture was already in the private sector under Communism.) In the CIS the private share is typically 15 to 30 per cent. Russia is more like Central Europe, as a result of the rapid voucher privatization of 1992–3.

Columns 2 and 3 show that privatization of small enterprises, particularly in the retail and service sectors, is more advanced than that of large-scale heavy industry. However, much private activity takes place in the shadow economy and is therefore unreported. This makes it hard to assess the amount of private enterprise. For example, in the Ukraine most of the private-sector activity is 'informal': formally the economy is almost entirely state-owned, though this may be about to change. Broad-based small-enterprise activity is greatest in the Czech Republic, Poland, Hungary and Bulgaria, with many hundreds of thousands of newly registered businesses. In Romania, agriculture has been completely privatized, with 2.4 million small private farmers. Generally speaking, the CIS countries lag far behind, with only forty active registered private companies in Tajikistan.

Enterprise and bank restructuring (including enterprise bankruptcies) are indicated in the fourth and last columns in Table 1. These show that only a limited amount has taken place, with few bankruptcies. Again, the Eastern European countries are ahead of the CIS.

The EBRD indicators show that price liberalization and price competition are now general, with only a few CIS countries lagging behind. The Eastern European countries, including the Baltic states, have abolished most of their import and export quotas and state control of foreign trade; most have achieved near current-account convertibility at unified exchange rates.

What about the 'tangible results'? The main indicators are real per-capita growth (proxy for improvements in living standards) and progress in macroeconomic stabilization, as measured by inflation rates. The EBRD data are presented in Table 2.

The first four columns show that over much of Eastern Europe the output falls which accompanied and followed the collapse of Communism have been reversed. In 1992 Poland became the first country to experience positive growth since the transition started. In 1993 Albania grew spectacularly, by 11 per cent, and Romania and Slovenia also recorded small positive growth rates. Recovery has followed large falls in output everywhere in 1991 and 1992: in the Baltic states the falls ranged from 26 to 38 per cent in 1992. (Of all the transition economies, the Czech Republic experienced the least disturbance to output and employment.) Real income is expected to go on falling in the CIS, though the pace of the decline has been moderated. The data almost certainly exaggerate the fall in output, since they mainly report the decline of the 'mega' industries and fail to report the growth of the 'informal' economy. Also, personal consumption has held up much better than output, since so much of the output was wasted. The new private sector has been the engine of growth in all post-Communist societies.

High rates of inflation mainly reflect the monetary financing of loss-making heavy industries, in the absence of adequate state revenue bases and bond markets. They are the macroeconomic counterpart of the lack of restructuring of enterprises and the financial system. Of the twenty-five post-Communist countries, seventeen experienced hyperinflation – inflation rates of more than 500 per cent a year – in 1992, fifteen of them in the CIS. In 1993 this was down to thirteen. In 1994, hyperinflation was experienced in only six. Apart from Poland (in 1989), Croatia, and the Baltic states, none of the Eastern European countries had hyperinflation. The current inflation rate in Albania, the Czech Republic, Croatia, Hungary, Latvia, Poland and the Slovak Republic is below 35 per cent annually, with the Czech Republic best with 10 per cent.

The EBRD report sums up as follows:

An 'advanced' group [of countries] consisting of the Czech Republic, Hungary, Poland, the Slovak Republic and Slovenia appear to be in the recovery phase and have achieved substantial structural reform and a large measure of macroeconomic stabilisation . . .

TABLE 2:   GROWTH AND INFLATION IN EASTERN
EUROPE AND THE FORMER SOVIET UNION

	REAL GDP (PERCENTAGE CHANGE)					RETAIL/CONSUMER PRICES (END-YEAR) (PERCENTAGE CHANGE)				
	1991	1992	1993	1994 (esti-mate)	1995 (projec-tion)	1991	1992	1993	1994 (esti-mate)	1995 (projec-tion)
Individual countries										
Albania	-27	-10	11	7	5	104	237	31	16	10
Armenia	-11	-52	-15	0	na	na	1341	10996	1100	na
Azerbaijan	-1	-23	-13	-22	-10	126	1395	810	1800	150
Belarus	-1	-10	-12	-22	-7	93	1558	1994	1875	300
Bulgaria	-12	-6	-4	0	4	339	79	64	122	70
Croatia	-14	-9	-3	1	4	149	937	1150	-3	3
Czech Republic	-14	-6	0	3	5	52	13	18	11	10
Estonia	-11	-14	-3	5	6	304	954	36	42	20
FYR Macedonia	-12	-14	-14	-7	0	115	1691	244	54	18
Georgia	-21	-43	-40	-35	na	131	1463	7492	7000	na
Hungary	-12	-4	-2	2	3	32	22	21	21	28
Kazakhstan	-13	-14	-12	-25	-12	150	1176	2169	1000	100
Kyrgyzstan	-5	-25	-16	-10	2	170	1771	1366	87	45
Latvia	-8	-34	-12	3	3	262	958	35	26	20
Lithuania	-13	-38	-16	2	4	345	1175	188	44	30
Moldova	-12	-29	-9	-25	0	162	2198	837	111	25
Poland	-8	2	4	5	5	60	44	38	30	23
Romania	-13	-14	1	3	3	223	199	296	62	40
Russia	-13	-19	-12	-15	-7	144	2318	841	205	100
Slovak Republic	-15	-7	-4	5	4	58	9	25	12	10
Slovenia	-8	-5	1	5	6	247	93	23	18	10
Tajikistan	-13	-34	-28	-25	na	204	1364	7344	-45	na
Turkmenistan	-5	-5	-10	-20	-5	155	644	9750	1100	500
Ukraine	-12	-17	-14	-23	2	161	2000	10155	401	120
Uzbekistan	-1	-11	-2	-3	-4	169	910	885	423	100
Aggregates										
Eastern Europe	-10	-4	1	3	4					
The Commonwealth of Independent States	-12	-19	-13	-17	-5					

Source: EBRD, *Transition Report*, April 1995 update, pp. 24–25

In an 'intermediate' group major stabilisation and reform efforts have been made but, so far, with mixed results. Some, such as Romania and Bulgaria, have been wrestling with macroeconomic stabilisation for some years but with only limited success . . . Albania and the Baltic states, despite suffering even greater falls in GDP, have also made great strides towards macroeconomic stabilisation and the reduction of inflation. Following earlier declines, Albania's economy grew rapidly in 1993, and sustained growth is in sight for Estonia, Latvia and Lithuania.

Other CIS countries have made considerably less progress. It is unlikely that the decline in recorded output in much of the CIS will be quickly arrested. Economic reform has been limited and inflation remains high.[3]

One reason for the divergence between the CIS and the rest is that the Communist system lasted longer in the Soviet Union than in its satellites: Balcerowicz in Poland had a two-year start on Gaidar in Russia. So it is not surprising that the satellites are 'ahead'. But this cannot be the whole explanation for the discrepancy: the Baltic countries have done much better, on every indicator, than the other successor states of the Soviet Union, while Romania and Bulgaria have done worse than the other former satellites. The countries best placed seem to be those with the longest previous experience of a market economy and/or those with the least time under Communist rule. Before Communism, Russia, Romania and Bulgaria were the least developed of the European capitalist states. The Central European and Baltic states fell under Communist rule later than the rest of the Soviet Union and missed the worst of Stalinism. The longer the experience of Communism, the harder it is to recover from it.

The economic data thus lend some support to the contentions of both Sachs and Gray. Shock therapy can achieve success, Poland being the most striking example. However, historical preconditions are also important, though whether they are decisive time will tell.

What of the politics? Sachs argues implicitly that rapid market-oriented reforms quickly create the political base to sustain them, whereas Gray appears to believe that legitimate political institutions are a prerequisite of market reforms: a finance minister, even if advised by Harvard, cannot do the job on his own. The Balcerowicz reforms in Poland were backed by the authority of Solidarity and Lech Wałęsa. Gray points to the striking comeback of neo-Communist parties, feeding off the pain of shock therapy. The politics of reinvention have given former Communists power or a share of power in seventeen of the twenty-five post-Communist states. Sachs counters that the key positions – usually the presidencies – in the post-Communist countries remain in the hands of anti-Communist reformers, that the restructured Communists are as keen as the anti-Communists to 'rejoin' Europe, that belief in Communism is dead, and that where neo-Communists retain or share power their support comes largely from the declining industry sectors, destined to rust away. All they can supply is a slowing-down mechanism, not any coherent alternative to marketization along capitalist lines.

Nevertheless, in discussing the political comeback of the Communists, Adam Karatynychky makes two telling points. The success of the former Communists, he says, has been greatly helped by the closure of Western European markets to the exports of the post-Communist countries and by the *economism* of the reform leaders. The reinvented Communists clawed their way back to power because the anti-Communists lost their moral voice. Instead of preaching democracy, liberty and spiritual values, all they talked about was rapid economic restructuring. Anti-Communism was hijacked by 'cold blooded economic surgeons'.[4] What this amounts to saying is that capitalism cannot create its own legitimacy – or at least not in the time it takes to deliver great material gains. This means that a successful transition to capitalism has to draw on a fund of moral capital, typically possessed by a leader who stood out courageously against the previous system. One can argue that it was the combination of Balcerowicz and Wałęsa in Poland

and of Klaus and Havel in the Czech Republic which was key to the success of the reforms in these two countries. But even such a combination may not be enough, as the faltering Gaidar-Yeltsin reform effort in Russia showed.

What has been achieved thus far in post-Communist societies is far from the normality of the West. But, as Klaus reminds us, 'Communism was so evil, so oppressive and so ineffective a system of government that no country which had suffered it could ever hope to move on and create a normally functioning society and economy until it has undergone a comprehensive and painful transformation. Such a change takes years to complete.'[5]

China is *sui generis*. It is post-Communist in several senses: its openness to the world, the growth of its private sector, the spectacular growth of its GDP. Since Deng Xiaoping started reforming the economy in 1978, China has become part of the 'East Asian miracle'. But it is still Communist in the literal sense of being ruled by the Communist Party. The Chinese economy is rigidly segmented into Communist and post-Communist parts. In essence, the hectic growth of the commercial sector in the countryside and the coastal enclaves pays for what is left of Communism. The question is: for how much longer will Chinese capitalists tolerate paying for the upkeep of a Communist party-state which cannot provide the public goods, particularly the financial infrastructure, needed for a market economy? And for how long will the emerging middle class which runs the private sector tolerate its lack of political representation? Liberalization from above has simply postponed the day of reckoning for the last major survivor of the collectivist nightmare.

The greatest threat to a peaceful and prosperous post-Communist future is economic collapse, territorial dissolution, and ethnic and religious wars in Russia and its 'near abroad'. The resulting black hole in the Eurasian heartland, still bristling with nuclear weapons, would be a profound danger to the peace of the world and the development of its economic life.

The economic data for the Russian Federation are summarized in Table 3.

So far as the statistics can be trusted, real GDP in Russia has fallen by over 40 per cent since the start of the reforms. The latest figures show that the decline may have bottomed out. The fall in living standards has been much less, and consumption has started to recover. Surveys of household spending show that in 1994 households bought about 80 per cent of the goods they did in 1991. Since they also grow more of their own food, and housing and heating are provided virtually free for most, living standards may not be worse than they were at the end of the Gorbachev era, though that is low enough – the average Russian wage is under $100 a month. However, there is evidence of a severe deterioration in health care, education and transport. The death rate has been rising, male life expectancy is falling, and infectious diseases – including diphtheria, cholera, syphilis, whooping cough and food poisoning – are all on the rise.

Unemployment has remained low, though this is set to rise. Rusting Russian firms have hung on to their workers like the dead souls in Gogol. Low unemployment suggests an absence of restructuring, though this may be exaggerated. Employment in Russian industry had fallen by 9 per cent by the end of 1993, but had increased rapidly in trade, financial services, and health care and education. By the end of 1993, 20 per cent of workers had changed jobs – exactly what should happen in restructuring. Nevertheless, the absence of state-provided social services – many services like housing and early schooling come with the job, and there is no national unemployment benefit system – is an obstacle both to labour mobility and to company profitability.

Inflation has come down from its hyperinflationary levels in 1992 and 1993, but is still running in treble figures. This reflects high monetary growth in the second half of 1994, mainly due to another wave of central-bank credits for heavy industry and agriculture. The bills for the Chechnya military operation have yet to be processed. Russia's obsolete industrial plant still churns out goods it cannot sell. Peter Karpov, deputy director of Russia's Federal Bankruptcy Agency, says, 'It is the product of our old system in which goods were traded according to the central plan, and money was like an amusing and insignificant little musical accompaniment.' As long as the industries have an open line to the central bank, hyperinflation can always return. An encouraging sign is that almost one thousand companies have been officially declared bankrupt, though only ten have been auctioned off.

As we have seen, privatization has been the big success of the reforms. By July 1994, 15,000 medium- and large-scale enterprises, employing over 70 per cent of the industrial workforce, had been privatized. Further cash-based sales of state enterprises to strategic investors are under way. By mid-1994 more than 70 per cent of state-owned small businesses in the retail trade, catering and consumer services had been privatized, and 30 per cent of all housing units were in private ownership. Today there are 700,000 registered small businesses operating in Russia. Many more are unregistered. This represents a large growth in new enterprises. Little progress has been made in privatizing agriculture, but there are over 300,000 small private farms which, occupying only 5 per cent of agricultural land, produce the largest share of many basic foodstuffs.

The main question mark over Russia today is the future of the state. Russia has been less a laboratory for shock therapy than a testing-ground for the theories of Hobbes. The shocks occurred because the state broke down. The breakdown has not been halted. The basic problem is the continuing erosion of the central state's fiscal base through tax evasion, criminality, fiscal separatism (the withholding of taxes by the republics and autonomous regions) and the flight from the rouble. The state's revenues have been shrinking ever since 1990. In 1994 the central government's share of official GDP came to only 13 per cent, which perhaps means not much more than 6 or 7 per cent

TABLE 3: THE RUSSIAN FEDERATION – SELECTED ECONOMIC DATA

	1989	1990	1991	1992	1993	1994 (Estimate)	1995 (Projection)
Output and expenditure			*(Percentage change)*				
Real GDP	na	na	-13	-19	-12	-15	-7
Real NMP	1.9	-4.0	-11.0	-20.0	-13	na	na
Investment at constant prices	4.1	0.1	-11.0	-45.0	-15.0	-27	na
Industrial production	1.4	-0.1	-8.0	-18.8	-16.0	-21	-12
Prices and wages							
Retail prices (annual average)	2.0	5.6	92.7	1354	896	220	na
Retail prices (end-period)	na	na	143.9	2318	841	205	100
Wages (annual average)	9.9	14.8	73.9	1065	885	na	na
Industrial wholesale prices (annual average)	1.2	3.9	138.1	1949	na	na	na
Industrial wholesale prices (end-period)	na	na	236.3	3275	1007	na	na
Monetary sector							
Credit to enterprises and households	na	na	127	803	452	na	na
Broad money (end-period)	14.6	17.6	126	643	416	170	na
Government sector			*(In percentage of GDP)*				
State budget balance (cash basis)	na	na	-16.0	-6.9	-5.7	na	na
General government balance (cash basis)	na	na	-31.0	-18.8	-8.0	-11.0	-8
External data			*(In billions of US dollars)*				
Current account balance vis-à-vis non-CIS countries (excl. gold)	na	-2.5	1.5	-1.7	6.2	na	na
Trade balance vis-à-vis non-CIS countries (excl. gold)	13.1	10.0	6.4	5.4	10.7	15.0	na
Gross external debt in convertible currencies (of the Soviet Union/Russia, end-period)	54.4	61.1	67.0	78.2	86.8	90	na
			(Percentage change)				
Exports to non-CIS countries (excl. gold)	8.5	0.8	-19.8	-16.7	9.0	8.4	na
Imports from non-CIS countries	13.8	7.3	-16.9	-16.8	-12.0	5.4	na
Miscellaneous items			*(Denomination as indicated)*				
Population (in millions, end-year)	147.6	148.3	148.9	148.6	148.3	148.2	na
Unemployment rate (in per cent of labour force, end-year)	0.0	0.0	0.1	0.8	1.1	2.1	na
Exchange rate (roubles per US$, end-year)	0.6	1.7	1.7	415.0	1247.0	3550	na
Exchange rate (roubles per US$, average)	0.6	na	1.7	222.0	930.0	2200	na
Refinancing rate	na	na	6 to 9	80	210	180	na
Nominal GDP (in billion roubles)	573	622	1130	14046	162300	650000	na
Nominal NMP (in billion roubles)	413	425	810	13100	120000	na	na
GNP per capita (in US dollars) at PPP exchange rates	na	na	na	na	5240	na	na

Source: EBRD, *Transition Report*, April 1995 update, pp. 24–25

of actual GDP collected. This is not enough to provide the public goods of law and order, administration, a sound monetary system, and payments for the army and social services. The dwindling of the state's authority in turn increases tax evasion, criminality, and so on.[6]

Part of what the state loses in revenue goes to the criminal gangs, the Russian *mafiosi*. There is no lack of gruesome semifacts to support the idea of a criminal take-over of Russia by sections of the old Communist *nomenklatura* and their armed retainers. An estimated 40 per cent of the turnover of goods and services is now controlled by organized crime; an estimated 100,000 criminals are organized in 3,000 to 4,000 gangs: the Russian murder rate is estimated at ten times that of the United States (itself no slouch). On 14 July 1994, the speaker of the Duma admonished members for coming into the chamber armed with handguns. More seriously, some of the gangs have been stealing and exporting military equipment, including parts of nuclear weapons scheduled for dismantling.

What makes the situation politically explosive is the interaction between criminality and territorial fragmentation. The republics and autonomous regions of the Russian Federation are bristling with weapons and soldiers, mostly outriders of the old Soviet army; civil wars rage in some of them. There are also 25 million ethnic Russians in the newly independent republics. There is an obvious temptation for the Russian government to try to restore 'law and order' and solve its fiscal crisis by rearming and reasserting control over parts of its old empire by force. This is the programme of Vladimir Zhirinovsky. Leaving imperial ambitions aside, how much disintegration can any state allow before attempting to assert its authority by force? This was the tragic choice facing Yeltsin in Chechnya. In attempting to reconquer the breakaway, criminalized republic, Yeltsin acted in character; but it may be that Russia will have to shed most of its Muslim population before its frontiers can be stabilized in a further unravelling of the empire acquired by the tsars.

For three years the Russian government has struggled unsuccessfully to bring the public finances under control in face of collapsing revenue and the insatiable demands of the military, industrial and agricultural lobbies. The collapse of the rouble in October 1994 precipitated sweeping changes in the government, the replacement of Gerashchenko as head of the central bank, and a new budget programme, backed, for the first time, by the IMF.

The budget for 1995, backed by an IMF stabilisation loan of $6.8 billion, could prove to be a turning point in Russia's fiscal policy. It forbids, for the first time, the monetary financing of a budget deficit projected at 5.6 per cent of GDP – the lowest since the 1980s. It is intended to reduce inflation to 1 per cent a month in the second half of the year. The budget has the status of law. This should help overcome the old problem of 'phone-call financing', where 'power' ministries would simply call their cronies in the Central Bank and get money.

The political situation for its fulfillment is also more favourable. The centre of political gravity has shifted from the old guard of 'red' directors and power ministries to the financiers, commercial banks and energy industry. These groups support the new political bloc 'Our-Home-Russia' which backs the prime minister. Russia's economic prospects are also promising. The fall in industrial production has bottomed out, and there are clearly great investment oportunities, with many industrial assets underpriced. Russia also has great export potential in oil, minerals, and raw materials. If stability can be achieved, capital flight, legal and illegal, should be reversed.

Belated Western support for Russia is the most hopeful outcome so far of the rouble crisis of October 1994. Western investment in the Russian state is demanded by hard-headed self-interest. For the same reason we should resist the clamour for an eastward expansion of NATO, and work out a pan-European security system embracing Russia and associated with the United States. The partnership for Peace is a step in the right direction. The pessimists urge us to keep up our guard, not to pour good money after bad, etc. But there is really no alternative to taking the gamble on the new Russia. That gamble must be made generously.

CHAPTER ELEVEN

REPAIRING THE STATE

The problem of state damage is not confined to the post-Communist world. The failures of collectivism everywhere led to the mistaken view that the state could do almost nothing and the market almost everything. Yet the theory of the liberal state is built on the concept of market failure. We need states because there are missing or failing markets. Keynes called these the 'gaps' in the *laissez-faire* system. There are missing markets in law and order; there are spillover (uncosted) effects of private actions – for example, the harms inflicted by polluting factories. A welfare state is needed because insurance markets are imperfect. There are failures in the markets for capital and labour. The existence of such gaps leaves scope for collective efforts to improve on spontaneous outcomes. Such collective efforts must be distinguished from collectivism – the doctrine that the state knows best. They are best seen as grants of authority and revenue to governments to produce goods which are generally wanted but which only governments can provide. In the reaction against collectivism, the existence of some of these imperfect markets was ignored.

One of the main gaps in classical liberal theory concerned the public goods needed for free trade. Nineteenth-century economists assumed that free trade, once established, would be easy to maintain since it conferred mutual advantages, and thus eliminated the chief causes of conflict. However, if there is large-scale unemployment the presumptions based on the theory of comparative advantage fall to the ground: the gain in employment from the imposition of import controls may easily outweigh losses caused by the resulting misallocation of resources. Moreover, once employment is in question, all the firms and industries 'losing out' from 'international competition' join the clamour for protection, and every nationalist tub-thumper can wax eloquent about the destruction of 'jobs' by 'foreigners'. Thus reasonable macroeconomic stability – stability of prices, employment, exchange rates – may be regarded as a necessary long-run condition of free trade. The Bretton Woods system, managed by the United States, provided such stability in the 1950s and 1960s. It made possible continuous trade liberalization, which in turn was a powerful factor in causing rapid output growth.

Since the 1970s the macroeconomy has been much less stable. The business cycle has returned, with large fluctuations in inflation, output, employment and exchange rates. At the same time, the economic rise of East Asia is commonly believed to have led to the destruction of many European and American manufacturing jobs. A combination of macroeconomic instability and rapid technical change has left the developed world with a legacy of long-term joblessness – whether reflected in unemployment statistics or rising inactivity rates. The poor have got relatively poorer. These, of course, were roughly the conditions which led to the rise of collectivism a hundred years ago, and, as then, the enthusiasm for free trade has notably declined. Few politicians are willing to advocate opening up their economies to low-cost competition from post-Communist countries. This is an ominous development, because the best contribution the West can make to the transition of former Communist countries to capitalism is to open up its markets to their goods.

As currently structured, the European Union is a major obstacle to the emergence of a Continental free-trade system. The 'Single Market', started in 1992, was the result of a deal whereby the nations of the then European Community agreed to open up *all* their markets to each other on condition that regulatory regimes, tax systems, monetary and fiscal rules, and social and environmental standards were standardized and harmonized across the Community to ensure 'fair competition'. Poorer countries and areas of the European Union also benefit from substantial fiscal transfers. The Maastricht Treaty capped the Single Market with an agreement to form a single-currency area. A European Union which opens up trade to countries which do not meet its standards deprives its members of the protections they have come to expect; if it accepts such countries as members, there will be substantial additional transfer obligations. The most important contribution the European Union could make to Europe's 'reunification' is to scrap the Common Agricultural Policy which supports small populations of high cost farmers at the expense of the European consumer and the former Soviet satellites.

Protectionist tendencies have, in any case, been powerfully strengthened by the long-term unemployment noted above. The free-trade impetus is not entirely dead: the Uruguay Round of the GATT, together with the setting-up of a new trade organization, is a notable attempt to extend global market integration from goods to financial services, foreign investment, multinational production and intellectual property. Nevertheless, the main trend since the 1970s has been towards protectionism, though this is difficult to quantify since so much of it takes the form of state-promoted cartels (market-sharing agreements) and anti-dumping and environmental regulations. The recent trend has been towards freer trade within blocs like the European Union and the North American Free Trade Area and 'managed' trade between them. The latter has been bolstered by fashionable 'strategic-trade' theory, which says that countries (and regions), like firms, should concentrate on their 'high-tech' winners in the battle of world markets. Since all cannot win, this kind of thinking tends to reduce trade to a zero-sum game: manufacturing job losses in Europe and the United States are widely, though wrongly, attributed to competition from East Asia. In the 1990s, writes Paul Krugman, 'the world is ripe for another outbreak of trade war'.[1]

The prospects for economic liberalism are thus tied up with the fuller or better utilization of resources, including human resources, in both Western Europe and the United States. Much of the current debate concerns the nature of the supply-side measures needed to bring this about. Without caricaturing too much, we are offered a choice between the American solution, based on labour-market flexibility, which has kept registered unemployment fairly low, and the European solution, based on large public investments in education and training and advanced infrastructure – for example, trans-European communications networks – designed to shrink long-term unemployment. Supply-side policy is a necessary ingredient for any durable recovery of previous activity levels. But it will take a long time to yield its fruits, and it does not guard against the danger of periodic economic collapse – not the best environment for trade liberalization.

The important name missing from these arguments is Keynes. Capitalist economies, he said, were unstable. If an economy suffers a shock, it does not simply return to its previous position: extra unemployment or underemployment develops and persists. Keynes brought in the state to stabilize the macroeconomy. By lowering interest rates or by increasing its own spending, the state could offset any tendency for private spending to fall.

Today this particular function of government is widely discredited. Financial markets, it is said, will not accept it. What they want from governments are sound money, sound finances, and low taxes. In a world of footloose capital, this financial discipline has become universal.

The financiers have a point. In the 1970s, Keynesian full-employment policy was associated with accelerating inflation and seemingly uncontrollable public-sector growth. The two were linked. The public sector was expanded to create or protect jobs; public-sector job creation was partly financed by inflation. By this means governments were able to fleece their creditors and reduce the real value of private saving. Moreover, as public spending across Western Europe climbed towards 50 per cent of national income, it started to look like socialism by stealth. The association of Keynesian policy with inflation and socialism destroyed it as a public good. If state financial policy is intended to stabilize the economy, it must not itself be a major source of instability.

The logic of the argument is that if we are to resist protectionism we must restore a financial system which excludes inflation while allowing the state to stabilize the business cycle. The best financial strategy for achieving this is one geared to keeping the growth of total money demand (cash spending or nominal GDP) in line with the growth of a country's productive capacity – neither more nor less. As Samuel Brittan and James Meade, both strong supporters of a money GDP target, have argued, this ensures reasonable price stability, while guarding against recessionary shocks, and thus combines the valid elements in both Keynesian and monetarist insights.[2] If the economy is inherently stable, as Friedman claimed, a nominal GDP target is equivalent to a price-level target (say zero inflation). If the economy is cyclically unstable, as Keynes claimed, a nominal GDP target allows measures to increase or decrease total money spending (including temporary budget deficits and surpluses) in the face of cyclical swings in output. What it excludes is the financing of inflationary wage settlements – wages rising ahead of productivity. It also excludes the use of budget deficits to raise the growth rate of the economy, as practised in the 1960s and early 1970s.

A world in which money incomes are stable will also tend to be a world of stable exchange rates. If the leading countries can maintain price stability for a few years, there is no reason why they should not commit themselves to keep exchange-rate fluctuations within narrow bounds, thus reinforcing domestic financial discipline. This would restore part of the Bretton Woods system missing since the collapse of the Smithsonian parities in 1973.

The financial rule needs to be supported by what I would call an 'anti-collectivist' rule designed to limit public spending as a share of national income. This is that public spending should not exceed 30 per cent of national income. There are two crucial economic arguments for such a rule. The first is that excessive public spending makes the economy less efficient and less productive, thus weakening the government's revenue base and increasing the likelihood of inflationary financing of spending programmes.

The second is that there is a limit to tax tolerance. Basing himself on data from the 1920s, Colin Clark in 1945 claimed that a tax/income ratio of above 25 per cent brought into being a pro-inflation coalition which aimed to reduce the government's real tax take back to 25 per cent.[3] It is likely that tax tolerance is now greater than it was in the 1920s; nevertheless, there is ample evidence that government spending policies ran into tax resistance in the 1970s, temporarily overcome by means of the inflation tax. Inflationary pressure was suppressed in turn by means of heavy unemployment. Clark's original insight was that the source of macroeconomic imbalances lies in the wrong relationship between the state and society. Quite simply, governments have been trying to do too much for the conditions of consent. In essence, the high tax regimes of Western Europe are now being maintained by high unemployment.

There is no correct tax/income ratio *a priori*. But a historical analysis similar to Colin Clark's would suggest that a sustainable tax/income ratio for developed countries – one consistent with stable prices and high employment – is in the range of 30 to 35 per cent. It is roughly what prevailed during the 'golden age' before inflation became a problem. And it is at the upper end of what governments of the newly developed and more dynamic economies of East Asia tax and spend today.

Getting down the share of taxes and public spending to anything approaching the 'golden' ratio has so far defeated the liberal-conservative revolution which swept the world in the 1980s – except in the post-Communist countries where state revenues simply collapsed.

Deep cuts in public spending and the taxes needed to finance it – cuts of the order of 10 to 20 per cent of national income – cannot be made without reducing the *social agenda* of the state. This has been extended far beyond the original welfare function, which was to provide a social safety net for those most at risk of misfortune and least able to protect themselves, into a system of universal entitlement to services which most of the population could now afford for themselves if they were not so heavily taxed. A reduction of the tax burden to nearer 30 than 50 per cent of national income would release a vast amount of private spending power for buying services which are now paid for by taxation, while leaving the state sufficient revenue to target help on those in need. It would also create a pattern of spending and saving which more closely approximates to what people want for themselves and their children.

How to achieve such cuts bristles with technical and political difficulties. But at root the issue is philosophical. We need to answer two kinds of questions. Are the welfare responsibilities which the state has assumed over this century any longer appropriate in privately wealthy societies? And what, in such societies, is the appropriate division of responsibility we would want to see between the individual and the state?

The state as spender is the last bastion of collectivism. The collectivist age will not be over until state spending has been drastically pruned. This pruning is the essential condition of the state as stabilizer of economies, which in turn is the best assurance of a liberal post-Communist world.

The adoption of a new financial framework is an integral part of what Hayek called the 'constitution of liberty'. It limits the state's exactions, and also creates more space for private responsibility and voluntary efforts. But there has also been a notable resurgence of liberalism as a *political* project, partly as a reaction to 'free-market fundamentalism', partly in response to the growth of administrative regulation. Markets and bureaucracy expanded in tandem in the 1980s, recalling Tocqueville and Max Weber, who saw individualism and despotism as twins. On the one hand, the spaces left vacant by the breakdown of corporatist bargaining were jointly filled by markets and the state. This has been most obvious in industrial relations, but it has happened in other areas – local government, education, health care, professional life. On the other hand, the privatization of public utilities has required tight regulatory regimes to replace loose accountability to national parliaments.

The problem is often seen as one of reinventing 'community' or 'civil society'. But it may be that marketization itself creates the voluntary associations needed to socialize it: firms and households will come together to pursue aims common to each. This is all to the good, provided free trade is rigorously upheld and no special privileges are granted by the state. Most proposals for constitutional reform aim at the classical liberal goals of strengthening individual rights against the state and dispersing power to elected lower-tier authorities. Newt Gingrich's 'Contract with America', endorsed in November 1994's midterm elections, aims to de-federalize American government. The European Union's 'subsidiarity' principle reflects this devolutionist strand in opposition to the statism of the Brussels bureaucracy. It would lead logically to a three-tier European Union, consisting of a weak federal centre, national governments, and regions. Germany, whose national state was delegitimized by past excesses, has been the main advocate of this conception of Europe – so far. British Conservatives have opposed it in the name of national sovereignty. Other European governments pay lip-service to the German vision (as locking the German state into a European structure), but it is not clear whether the French will want to reduce national states to the status of state governments in a new federation. Absorbing the post-Communist countries of Central Europe into an expanded European system and reconciling rediscovered national and regional identities with effective central institutions will test political inventiveness for years to come.

The main strands of the discussion can now be drawn together. Fukuyama's vision of the 'universal, homogeneous state', united by free-trade economics and political democracy, is a pipedream: large parts of Asia and Africa will not conform, as John Gray points out. Cultural separateness, however, need not lead to economic isolation. Liberal economics is culture-blind, and can be a powerful integrating and pacifying force, so long as it is not expected to produce a standardized culture and common political and social institutions: Sachs is right to say that the 'core institutions' of capitalism can be, and have been, implanted the world over, to take root in their culturally differentiated habitats.

We are left with the task of reviving 'the Western project' for those countries which are part of the historic West, including the European diaspora. The Western project is liberal, though this must not be exclusively identified with individualism – liberalism has its roots in feudalism as well as in individualism and nationalism. It is compatible with social democracy, though not with socialism, which has never won popular endorsement in the West. Whenever the socialist project has threatened to overstep the bounds of social democracy it has been repelled by the intellectual traditions and social habits of free peoples.

The great question is whether Russia is part of the West or the non-West. It is the one European country which has succumbed to full-blooded collectivism without outside help, though only under postwar conditions of catastrophic state collapse and social chaos. Western European civilization could produce a Marx or a Hitler, but not a Lenin or a Stalin. Soviet Communism was never part of the Western project – not even a deviant branch of it – but more akin to Asiatic despotism. Yet Russia has cast off this alien system almost bloodlessly. Its present leadership is overwhelmingly 'Western' in orientation. We cannot afford to see this great nation, shorn of its pride, slide into anarchy and despair. If through inattention, selfishness or narrow economic calculation we stand aside, we doom our own best hopes.

The practical task of a revived liberal project is to repair state damage after the ravages of collectivism. In Russia this means equipping the central government with the resources to enable it to provide the basic public goods of a liberal state; in Western Europe it means restoring the state's credibility as an economic manager.

The passing of Communism is regretted by some, but it

should not be. In its heroic phase – in Russia in the 1930s, in China in the 1950s and 1960s – it inflicted immense damage on the people it ruled. In its decrepitude it was merely oppressive, stagnant and stultifying. Its passing – and that of the Cold War – has given rise to all kinds of new problems and revived many old ones. But they are nothing when weighed in the balance against the liberation of freedom, energy and opportunity.

It is more important to be reminded of what we have gained than of what we have lost. Capitalist democracies do not commit evil – certainly not systematically. As Raymond Aron once wrote, their defects are 'sins of omission' rather than of 'commission'. The United States and its allies killed tens of thousands in defending freedom: the Communist countries killed tens of millions in promoting socialism. This disparity is not fortuitous: it stems from the inherent difference between an open and a closed system of thought and politics. The arguments will continue about where to draw the borders of the state, and about how much equality is compatible with liberty. But a democratic state in which civil and political rights are entrenched, which provides the public good of economic stability, and which spends no more than 30 per cent of GDP is one that could enable a great deal of good and do comparatively little harm.

REFERENCES

CHAPTER ONE

1. Alistair Horne, *Macmillan, 1957–1986* (1989), p. 303
2. Quoted in Martin Walker, *The Cold War and the Making of the Modern World* (1993), p. 114
3. Ibid., p. 115
4. *Washington Post*, 20 December 1957; quoted in Walker, op. cit., p. 115
5. Quoted in Walker, op. cit., pp. 131–2
6. Ibid., p. 77
7. For example Brian Thomas's essay in David Carlton and Herbert M. Levine (eds.), *The Cold War Debated* (1988)
8. Quoted in Walker, op. cit., p. 150
9. Ronald Reagan, *An American Life* (1990), p. 13
10. Ibid., pp. 237–8
11. Ibid., p. 549

CHAPTER TWO

1. A. V. Dicey, *Introduction to the Study of the Law of the Constitution* (1914 edn), p. lxxiii
2. F. A. Hayek, *The Road to Serfdom* (1944), p. 56
3. For the roots of the French Revolution in 'aristocratic resurgence', see R. R. Palmer, *The Age of the Democratic Revolution*, vol. 1 (1959), esp. chs 2–4
4. Quoted in L. Siedentop, *Tocqueville* (1994), p. 91
5. See R. M. Page in N. F. R. Crafts and Nicholas Woodward (eds), *The British Economy since 1945* (1991), pp. 490–1

6. Colin Croch and Ronald Dore (eds), *Corporatism and Accountability* (1993), p. 3
7. Ibid., p. 6
8. Hayek, op. cit., p. 61

CHAPTER THREE

1. A. J. P. Taylor, *English History 1914–1945* (1965), pp. 1–2
2. John Hicks, *A Theory of Economic History* (1969), pp. 22–4
3. Friedrich List, *National System of Political Economy* (Eng. ed. 1885), pp. 368, 176–7, 145
4. Emil Davies, *The Collectivist Society in the Making* (1914), p. xiv
5. Quoted in James Gilbert, *Designing the Industrial State: The Intellectual Pursuit of Collectivism in America 1880–1940* (1972), p. 34
6. K. Polanyi, *The Great Transformation* (1944), p. 251
7. The classic text is V. I. Lenin, *Imperialism* (1917). His invention came out of the pre-war debate with the German revisionist Karl Kautsky
8. Quoted in M. Walker, *The Cold War and the Making of the Modern World* (1993), p. 44
9. Quoted in *Historical Precedents for Economic Change in Central Europe and the USSR*, Oxford Analytica/CSFB, 1991, p. 7
10. G. Barraclough, *An Introduction to Contemporary History* (1964), p. 44
11. Ibid., p. 54
12. J. A. Hobson, quoted in P. Clarke, *Liberals and Social Democratics* (1978), p. 138
13. E. J. Hobsbawm, *Labouring Men* (1964), p. 258
14. Robert A. Nisbet, *The Sociological Tradition* (1966), p. 24
15. Quoted in Arthur Schlesinger, *The Imperial Presidency* (1974), p. viii
16. D. G. Ritchie, quoted in Michael Freeden, *The New Liberalism* (1978), p. 98
17. J. M. Keynes, *The Economic Consequences of the Peace* (1919), in *Collected Writings* vol. 2, pp. 6–7

CHAPTER FOUR

1. For the inflation tax, see J. M. Keynes, *Collected Writings*, vol. iv, ch. 3

2. Arthur Salter, *Recovery* (1932), p. 241

3. B. Mussolini, *Fascism: Doctrine and Institutions* (1935), pp. 7–31

4. E. H. Carr, *The Russian Revolution from Lenin to Stalin* 1917–1929 (1979), p. 36

5. J. M. Keynes, *Collected Writings*, vol. xvii, pp. 393–4

6. J. M. Keynes, *Collected Writings*, vol. xi, pp. 262–6; vol. xviii, pp. 404–5

7. John Toye, 'Keynes, Russia and the State in Developing Countries', in Tony Thirlwall and Derek Crabtree (eds), *Keynes and the Role of the State* (1993)

8. Charles Maier, *Recasting Bourgeois Europe* (1975), pp. 9, 15

9. Carr, op. cit., p. 152

10. Tom Bottomore, *The Socialist Economy, Theory and Practice* (1990), p. 35

11. J. M. Keynes, *Collected Writings*, vol. ix, p. 352

12. J. M. Keynes, *Collected Writings*, vol. ii, pp. 9–10

13. Charles P. Kindleberger, *The World in Depression 1929–1939* (1973), p. 83

14. Kindleberger, op. cit., p. 292

15. Raymond Carr, *Times Literary Supplement*, 26 August 1994

16. John A. Garraty, *The Great Depression* (1986), ch. 8

17. Ibid., p. 169

18. Quoted in Loren J. Okroi, *Galbraith, Harrington and Heilbroner: Economics and Dissent in an Age of Optimism* (1986), p. 32

19. A. G. B. Fisher, *Economic Self-Sufficiency* (Royal Institute of International Affairs, 1939), p. 22

20 Leo Amery, *The Forward View* (1934), ch. 2

21. G. D. H. Cole, 'Planning International Trade', in *Foreign Affairs*, 1934

22. See Lionel Robbins, *Economic Planning and International Order* (1937)

23. Walter Lippmann, 'Self-Sufficiency: Some Random Reflections',

Carnegie Endowment for International Peace, Documents for the Year, 1934

CHAPTER FIVE

1. G. Allen, *Japan's Economic Recovery* (1958), p. 33
2. J. M. Keynes, *Collected Writings*, vol. ix, p. 291; vol. vii, pp. 379–80
3. J. M. Keynes, *Collected Writings*, vol. xxii, p. 123
4. J. M. Keynes, *Collected Writings*, vol. xxii, pp. 620, 624
5. For a good account of the Beveridge principles, see Andrew Dilnot's essay, ch. 11, in Dieter Helm (ed.), *The Economic Borders of the State* (1989)
6. Sidney and Beatrice Webb, *The Decay of Capitalist Civilisation* (1923), p. 26
7. See Enrico Barone's 'The Ministry of Production in a Collectivist State' and Ludwig von Mises's 'Economic Calculation in the Socialist Commonwealth', reprinted in F. A. Hayek, *Collectivist Economic Planning* (1935)
8. Hayek, op. cit.
9. For Dobb, see the summary in Wlodzimierz Brus, *The Market in a Socialist Economy* (1964), pp. 35–40; Hayek's comment in Hayek, op. cit., pp. 215–16
10. F. A. Hayek, *The Road to Serfdom* (1944), pp. 221–2, 105
11. Ibid., p. 107
12. Ibid., p. 41
13. Ibid., p. 36
14. Ibid., p. 122
15. J. M. Keynes, *Collected Writings*, vol. xxvii, pp. 385–8
16. Hayek, *The Road to Serfdom*, pp. 207–8
17. Andrew Dilnot, in Helm, op. cit., p. 242
18. N. F. R. Crafts and Nicholas Woodward (eds), *The British Economy since 1945* (1991), pp. 7–8
19. W. Rostow, *Getting from Here to There* (1978), ch. 2
20. Ben Pimlott, *Harold Wilson* (1992), p. 218
21. R. Crossman, *Re-Thinking Socialism 1951–1964* (1965), pp. 120f.

22. I. M. D. Little et al., *Boom, Crisis and Adjustment: The Macroeconomic Experience of Developing Countries* (1993), p. 26
23. Quoted in *World Development Report 1991* (World Bank), p. 34
24. M. Duverger, quoted in Alfred G. Meyer, 'Theories of Convergence', in C. Johnson (ed.), *Change in Communist Systems* (1970), p. 322
25. D. Riesman, *State and Welfare, Tawney, Galbraith and Adam Smith* (1982), pp. 152–3
26. S. Brittan, *The Economic Consequences of Democracy* (1977), p. 5
27. Quoted in L. Malabre Jr, *Lost Prophets* (1993), p. 77
28. President's Council of Economic Advisers, March 1961, quoted in Herbert Stein, *The Fiscal Revolution in America* (1969), p. 398
29. R. Bacon and Walter Eltis, *Britain's Economic Problem: Too Few Producers* (1976), p. 93
30. Alan Coddington, *Keynesian Economics: The Search for First Principles* (1983), pp. 42–3
31. M. Ellman. *Collectivism, Convergence and Capitalism* (1984), p. 169

CHAPTER SIX

1. János Kornai, *The Socialist System: The Political Economy of Communism* (1992), p. 362
2. Quoted in Alec Nove, *The Economics of Feasible Socialism* (1983), p. 198
3. F. A. Hayek (ed.), *Collectivist Economic Planning* (1935), pp. 204–5; for an account of the Lange–Lerner model, see the entry under 'Lange–Lerner Mechanism' in *The New Palgrave: A Dictionary of Economics*, ed. John Eatwell, Murray Milgate and Peter Newman (1987)
4. At the Twentieth Party Congress in February 1956
5. Kornai, op. cit., p. 167
6. Hayek, op. cit.
7. Mark Harrison, 'Soviet Economic Growth since 1928: The Alternative Statistics of G. I. Khanin', in *Europe–Asia Studies*, vol. 45, no. 1 (1993), p. 142
8. P. A. Samuelson, *Economics* (8th edn 1970), p. 830
9. G. I. Khanin and V. Selyunin, 'The Elusive Figure', *Novy Mir*;

translated in *The Current Digest of the Soviet Press*, vol. 39, no. 25 (1987), pp. 10–12

10. R. Erikson, 'The Soviet Statistical Debate: Khanin versus TsSU' in H. Rowen and C. Wolf (eds), *The Impoverished Superpower: Perestroika and the Soviet Military Burden* (1990), p. 71

11. Kornai, op. cit., pp. 302–3, 308–9; Timothy Garton Ash, *The Uses of Adversity: Essays on the Fate of Central Europe* (1989), p. 8

12. Quoted in Anders Åslund, *Gorbachev's Struggle for Economic Reform* (1991 edn), p. 19

13. Kornai, op. cit., p. 315

14. Ibid., pp. 318–28

15. G. Breslauer, *Khrushchev and Brezhnev as Leaders* (1983), p. 54

16. Quoted in M. Ellman, *Collectivisation, Convergence and Capitalism* (1984), p. 304

17. Åslund, op. cit., p. 155

18. Ibid., p. 13

19. Yedor Gaidar, Lionel Robbins Memorial Lectures, LSE, 4–6 May 1993, p. 12. Transcribed notes

20. In the famous Novosibirsk Report, leaked extracts of which were first published in the West in the *Washington Post*, 3 August 1983, and the *New York Times*, 5 August 1993

21. Quoted, from 1991, in R. V. Daniels, *The End of the Communist Revolution* (1993), pp. 13–14

22. Ibid., p. 17

23. Åslund, op. cit., p. 221.

CHAPTER SEVEN

1. J. M. Keynes, *Collected Writings*, vol. iv, p. 37

2. Quoted in *World Development Report* (World Bank, 1991), p. 139

3. For a useful analysis along these lines see A. Gamble and P. Walton, *Capitalism and the State* (1976), p. 185

4. Anthony King et al., *Why is Britain Becoming Harder to Govern?* (1976), pp. 18–19

5. Charles Lindblom, *Politics and Markets* (1977), pp. 98, 349

6. R. E. Pahl and J. T. Winkler, 'The Coming Corporatism', in *New*

Society, 10 October 1974; Winkler quoted in R. Skidelsky (ed.), *The End of the Keynesian Era* (1977), p. 79

7. Fred Hirsch's essay in Fred Hirsch and John G. Goldthorpe (eds), *The Political Economy of Inflation* (1977), pp. 269–80

8. M. Friedman and R. Friedman, *Free To Choose* (1980), p. 283

9. See James Buchanan, 'From Private Preferences to Public Philosophy: The Development of Public Choice', in *IEA Readings*, 18 (1978), pp. 3–20

10. See Deepak Lal, *Fighting Fiscal Privilege: Towards a Fiscal Constitution* (Social Market Foundation, 1990)

11. A. O. Hirschman, *Exit, Voice and Loyalty* (1970), p. 4

12. Ibid., ch. 4

13. David Howell, *Blind Victory: A Study in Income, Wealth and Power* (1986), p. 4

14. J. Toleday and S. Zeitlin, *The Automobile and Its Workers – Between Fordism and Flexibility* (1987), pp. 17–18

15. *The OECD Jobs Study, Unemployment in the OECD area 1950–1995* (1994), p. 36

16. F. A. Hayek, *Daily Telegraph*, 16 October 1974

17. In R. Skidelsky (ed.), *Thatcherism* (1988), pp. 55–6

18. Quotations from Ronald Reagan, *An American Life* (1990), pp. 105, 66–7, 119, 185, 189, 139, 142, 201, 205, 226–7

19. Quotations from Hugo Young, *One of Us* (1989), pp. 5, 84, 103–4, 120, 123

20. Margaret Thatcher, *The Downing Street Years* (1993), pp. 14–15

21. Shirley Letwin, *The Anatomy of Thatcherism* (1992), ch. 2

22. For the details of Reagan's macroeconomic policy, see the introductory essay by Martin Feldstein in Martin Feldstein (ed.), *American Economic Policy in the* 1980s (1994); the quotation is from Michael Prowse, *Financial Times*, 4 August 1994

23. A. O. Hirschman, *Essays in Trespassing* (1981), p. 110

24. Jeffrey Sachs, letter to the author, 2 August 1994

CHAPTER EIGHT

1. C. F. Pratten, 'Mrs Thatcher's Economic Experiment', in *Lloyd's Bank Review*, January 1982, p. 40

2. S. Fischer and A. Gelb, 'Issues in Socialist Market Reform', in P. Marer and S. Zecchini (eds), *The Transition to a Market Economy in Central and Eastern Europe* (1991), p. 184

3. Jeffrey Sachs, *Poland's Jump to the Market Economy* (1993), p. 28

4. Ibid., p. 54

5. Quoted in John Morrison, *Boris Yeltsin* (1991), p. 44

6. Ibid., p. 161

7. Boris Yeltsin, *The View from the Kremlin* (1994), p. 18

8. Ibid., pp. 168, 200

9. Yegor Gaidar, 'Inflationary Pressures and Economic Reform in the Soviet Union', in P. H. Admiral (ed.), *Economic Transition in Eastern Europe* (1993), p. 83

10. Yegor Gaidar, Lionel Robbins Memorial Lectures, LSE, 4–6 May 1993, p. 30. Transcribed notes

11. Ibid., p. 26

12. Ibid., p. 35

13. Ibid., p. 37

14. Andres Köves, *Central and East European Economies in Transition* (1992), p. 38

15. Maxim Boycko, Andrei Shleifer and Robert W. Vishny, 'Mass Privatization in Russia' (typescript, 1993), p. 14

16. Ibid., p. 20

17. Yeltsin, op. cit., p. 193

18. Ibid., p. 205

19. For Yavlinsky, see R. Skidelsky (ed.), *Russian Reforms: Analysis and Debate*, IRIS/SMF, October 1995; for Glasyev, 'Stabilization? Nonsense', *Moscow Times*, International Weekly Edition, 2 July 1995.

CHAPTER NINE

1. D. Moynihan, *Pandaemonium: Ethnicity in International Politics* (1993), p. 15

2. Jacques Rupnik, 'Europe's New Frontiers: Remapping Europe', in *Daedalus*, Summer 1994, p. 93

3. Francis Fukuyama, 'The End of History', in *The National Interest*,

Summer 1989; *The End of History and the Last Man* (1992) is the extended and revised book version

4. John Gray, *London Review of Books*, 22 September 1994
5. John Gray, *The Undoing of Conservatism* (Social Market Foundation, 1994), p. 19
6. See Tony Judt, 'Nineteen Eighty-nine: The End of *Which* European Era?', in *Daedalus*, Summer 1994, p. 17
7. John Gray, *Post-Communist Societies in Transition: A Social Market Perspective* (Social Market Foundation, 1994)
8. The quotations which follow are from Jeffrey Sachs, *Understanding Shock Therapy* (Social Market Foundation, 1994)
9. Mark Medish, 'Russia: Lost and Found', in *Daedalus*, Summer 1994, pp. 64–71

CHAPTER TEN

1. Václav Klaus, *The Economist*, 19 September 1994
2. *Transition Report: Economic Transition in Eastern Europe and the former Soviet Union* (EBRD, 1994)
3. Ibid., p. 147
4. In the *National Review*, 27 June 1994
5. Klaus, op. cit.
6. Jeffrey Sachs, 'Russia's Struggle with Stabilization: Conceptual Issues and Evidence', paper prepared for the World Bank's Annual Conference on Development Economics, Washington, DC, 28–29 April 1994, pp. 41–6. See also *Russian Economic Trends*, 1995; vol. 4.1, p. 18.

CHAPTER ELEVEN

1. See Paul Krugman, *Peddling Prosperity* (1994), p. 288
2. Samuel Brittan, *Capitalism with a Human Face* (1995), p. 177; James Meade, *Full Employment without Inflation* (Employment Policy Institute/Social Market Foundation, 1994)
3. Colin Clark, 'Public Finance and Changes in the Value of Money', *Economic Journal*, vol. 60, 1945

INDEX